explore
the Northeast
National Marine Sanctuaries
WITH JEAN-MICHEL COUSTEAU

explore
the Northeast
National Marine Sanctuaries
WITH JEAN-MICHEL COUSTEAU

THUNDER BAY | STELLWAGEN BANK | MONITOR

OCEAN PUBLISHING

Copyright © 2013 by Ocean Futures Society

ISBN 978-0-9826940-3-9

Book cover, layout and design by Nate Myers, Wilhelm Design
Editing by Dr. Maia McGuire

Printed in the United States of America

Front Cover: Ocean Futures Team Members, L-R Blair Mott, Matthew Ferraro and Chuck Davis, prepare to dive in Stellwagen Bank.
Photo Credit: Carrie Vonderhaar, Ocean Futures Society

10 9 8 7 6 5 4 3 2 1

Praise for

Explore the National Marine Sanctuaries with Jean-Michel Cousteau

"This book series gives us deeply felt and profound insight into our country's amazing National Marine Sanctuaries. They are wonderful, illuminating volumes that show the sanctuaries' great beauty and awe. There is an urgent need for the world to learn about these momentous marine sanctuaries and how to protect them. I thank my dear friend, Jean-Michel Cousteau, and Ocean Futures Society, for calling attention to the care of these beautiful marine sanctuaries in our time of extreme need. Jean-Michel is the authoritative servant on the sea for our generation and future generations. This incredible series will be beneficial in getting the word out about the importance of protecting our oceans and the marine life that call it home."

> Robert Lyn Nelson
> Artist/Environmentalist

"Jean-Michel Cousteau and Ocean Futures Society have set themselves the task of communicating the beauty of the ocean and the necessity of protecting it to the widest possible audience. Through stunning photography and superbly succinct writing, Explore the National Marine Sanctuaries with Jean-Michel Cousteau *does just that. This wonderful book series shows how very precious the USA's National Marine Sanctuaries are, and what a huge contribution the sanctu-*

aries make to our knowledge and understanding of the underwater world. The series is also very timely in light of recent events in the Gulf of Mexico which show how vulnerable the marine environment still is. Oil spillages do not respect marine sanctuaries any more than forest fires respect the boundaries of National Parks.

But without even the protection that the National Marine Sanctuaries offer, America's marine biodiversity—and the public knowledge and appreciation of it—would be the poorer. Those of us whose lives revolve around the protection of wildlife on land, rather than the marine environment, can only admire and envy Jean-Michel's extraordinary success in conserving, communicating and educating. Genuine environmentalists like Jean-Michel know that we need a truly holistic approach to the conservation of wildlife on land and sea. This book series is an undoubted 'treasure-house' and I have no hesitation in recommending it to all who love wildlife and wish to understand better how to redress the terrible imbalance between Man and Nature."

Simon Cowell, MBE FRGS MCIJ
Founder, Wildlife Aid; Producer and
Presenter, Wildlife SOS, United Kingdom

"Marine sanctuaries represent the most special places in the ocean. We cannot sustain the ocean without first sustaining our sanctuaries. But like all things in the ocean, they are beneath the surface and invisible to almost everyone. Jean-Michel, through his films and this book series, gives these life and makes the ocean visible and tangible. He is a keen observer of nature and a storyteller about the ocean. He adds a depth of understanding and interpretation that is easy for everyone to grasp."

Daniel J. Basta, Director
NOAA's Office of National Marine Sanctuaries

"Jean-Michel Cousteau and his team have put together an amazing series of books dedicated to the undersea world on which we depend. This is the first time anyone has truly captured the experience of diving America's underwater treasures, the entire national marine sanctuary system. I cannot tell you how truly beautiful and moving a series this is. After spending time with this book, I am even more proud of America's commitment to protect our National Marine Sanctuaries."

Jeff Mora, Los Angeles Lakers, Executive Chef,
Board Member, National Marine Sanctuary Foundation
International Advisory Board Member, Ocean Futures Society

"National Marine Sanctuaries are not only extraordinary places to visit, they are also one of our most powerful tools in ocean conservation. Explore the National Marine Sanctuaries with Jean-Michel Cousteau provides an underwater roadmap through the Sanctuaries with compelling stories and magnificent images. For those fortunate enough to have visited Sanctuaries, these books are the perfect way to preserve the memories. For those who have not, they are the next best thing to being there. Most importantly, Explore the National Marine Sanctuaries with Jean-Michel Cousteau teaches us that by protecting National Marine Sanctuaries we help protect the world-ocean...and ourselves."

Bob Talbot, Chairman of the Board,
National Marine Sanctuary Foundation;
Board of Directors, Sea Shepherd Conservation Society,
Filmmaker and Photographer

Contents

Foreword

Jean-Michel Cousteau's love of the ocean and the desire to protect it began as a boy, inspired by living on the edge of the Mediterranean Sea and sharing underwater adventures in the Atlantic, Pacific and Indian oceans with his parents, brother, and other pioneering ocean explorers aboard the legendary ship, *Calypso*. Ask him what it is about the ocean that has captured his heart and mind, and he might tell you of face-to-face encounters with curious fish, squid and great white sharks or the joy of gliding through forests of kelp or being underwater at night surrounded by a living cosmos of bioluminescent creatures. He could say how rewarding it is to be an explorer, to be the first to see places and meet forms of life in the sea that have not yet been given names. And, he would likely encourage you to go experience such things for yourself in places such as those celebrated in this volume and others that follow.

Cousteau's deep commitment to the National Marine Sanctuary Program stems from understanding how important the sanctuaries are as a means of protecting the nation's natural, historic and cultural heritage. Like national parks and wildlife management areas on the land, marine sanctuaries safeguard healthy systems and help restore those that have been harmed. While some observers believe the ocean should be able to take care of itself, many species prized for food or sport have declined by 90 percent or more in a few decades. Low oxygen areas, "dead zones," are proliferating, and sea grass meadows and coral reefs are diminishing. Major changes, most not favorable to humankind, are underway, and the sanctuaries can give stressed systems and species a break. We need the oceans, and now the oceans need us to do what it takes to restore health to the world's blue heart.

I share with Jean-Michel Cousteau the delight of being sprayed with whale breath at Stellwagen Bank, dodging sea turtles while looking for fossils of ice age animals at Gray's Reef off the coast of Georgia, of gliding among giant parrotfish in the Florida Keys, and immersing myself in a blizzard of eggs from spawning coral at the Flower Garden Banks off the coasts of Texas and Louisiana. There is haunting beauty and mystery in the protected shipwrecks lying within the Great Lakes, and others such as the remains of the Civil War vessel, *Monitor*, once a home for sailors, now a sanctuary for clouds of small fish and large grouper.

Those who visit any of California's four National Marine Sanctuaries have a chance to glimpse blue whales, the largest animals on earth, as well as some of the smallest, the minute planktonic creatures that drive ocean food webs. The Olympic National Marine Sanctuary holds healthy kelp forests adjacent to stands of ancient trees, and westward, in the Hawaiian Islands, special protection is being provided for some notable annual visitors, humpback whales. Coral reefs and the enormous diversity of life they contain are valued – and protected – in the Northwest Hawaiian Islands, American Samoa and a series of reefs, atolls and deep canyons near the Mariana Islands. These are all vital parts of the nation's treasury, places that give hope for the ocean, and therefore hope for ourselves.

I am pleased to be associated with the Ocean Futures Society, the organization Jean-Michel Cousteau founded to explore, communicate discoveries and messages to people and inspire them to take action to restore and protect the living ocean. They are making a difference – and so can you. Your reading of this book series is a strong first step in your understanding of the importance of protecting the sanctuaries for generations to come.

Dr. Sylvia Earle
Oakland, California

Preface

Over four decades have passed since the U.S. Congress had the foresight to create the National Marine Sanctuary System. It was the beginning of an era when the general public was becoming increasingly aware that the environment was under siege and protection was needed while we tried to figure out what was going wrong. Among the things we've learned since then is that creating protected areas is part of doing what's right.

NOAA's mission with the sanctuary systems was "…to serve as the trustee for the nation's system of marine protected areas, to conserve, protect, and enhance their biodiversity, ecological integrity and cultural legacy." The site chosen for the first sanctuary was unusual: one-square-mile of ocean 16 miles offshore and at 230 feet of depth. It was intended to preserve a piece of history, a cultural legacy, embodied in the wreck of the Civil War Ironclad USS *Monitor*, found over 100 years after it sank. It is the only sanctuary dedicated to the preservation of a single cultural treasure.

This volume of the *Explore the National Marine Sanctuaries with Jean-Michel Cousteau* series is full of the adventure of finding, exploring and protecting the *Monitor*, but it also contains an exploration of the water-borne history of an entire nation through other shipwrecks and the history of exploitation and transformation of natural resources that could only be told at the Thunder Bay and Stellwagen Bank Sanctuaries.

Unlike the site of the *Monitor*, several of the over 200 sunken vessels at the Thunder Bay Sanctuary in Lake Huron, Michigan, are accessible to sports divers and our Ocean Futures Society team was among the most enthusiastic. It was also a challenge because this is the only freshwater Sanctuary and that alters some of the physics of diving. The waters of this Sanctuary contain a history that spans over 12,000 years of trade and settlement by boat, in what became one of the world's most active waterways. The number of shipwrecks lost to sometimes harsh and unpredictable elements is told here, but it is also the range and diversity of vessels that details the story of a growing nation.

The challenge that the mission of the Sanctuary System faces "to conserve and protect" is also detailed here as a reminder that conditions in nature alter unpredictably, creating change we are sometimes slow to perceive. Lake Huron, parts of the Sanctuary, and now each of the Great Lakes have been subjected to an upheaval caused by invasive species, specifically, the effects of the zebra mussel invasion, a species introduced from the ballast water of ships containing this mussel which originates from the Balkans, Poland and the former Soviet Union. So the marine sanctuary system is not only a microcosm of water systems found throughout the world, it is a laboratory indicating how the world is connected and constantly changing and adapting.

The third National Marine Sanctuary covered in this volume is the Gerry E. Studds Stellwagen Bank Sanctuary, named both for the explorer who first described the rising plateau of its fertile bank and the Congressman who championed it as a protected area. At the mouth of Massachusetts Bay, this sanctuary hosts some of the most boisterous and plentiful marine life and spans historic shipping and fishing grounds that helped define a new nation and its early centers at Boston, Gloucester, Plymouth, Salem, and Provincetown. The long-lasting fishing boom on cod and its eventual demise took place in these waters. Whaling boats set sail from here in the era when a successful whaling voyage was the marine equivalent of striking gold.

Whaling vessels have transformed into a whale-watching industry and, with continued protection and research, these waters will continue to thrive with whales and fish, and new histories will be written.

Each of these protected areas is both unique and emblematic of marine richness and human history. The existence of these waters as Sanctuaries brings great promise that, with inevitable and unpredictable change, the richness they contain will flourish. But we must pay continued and intelligent attention.

I invite you to be part of that adventure and to uncover, page by page, in this volume the exhilaration of exploring these treasures of the sea.

Jean-Michel Cousteau
Santa Barbara, California

Introduction

About this Series

The four-book series, *Explore the National Marine Sanctuaries with Jean-Michel Cousteau*, has been developed in partnership with the National Marine Sanctuary system and Ocean Futures Society. Text in *italics* is excerpted from the previously-published (2007), limited-edition book *America's Underwater Treasures* by Jean-Michel Cousteau and Julie Robinson with photography by Carrie Vonderhaar. That book describes the experience and research of Jean-Michel and his Ocean Futures Team while diving all 13 underwater marine sanctuaries and the one underwater marine monument. Their experiences are captured in a film by the same name aired on PBS as part of *Jean-Michel Cousteau's Ocean Adventures*. The current series is offered to make information on these vital sanctuaries even more inclusive for the American public.

Each book in the series takes readers to one of the four regions of the country into which NOAA has organized its management of the National Marine Sanctuaries. This book, *Explore the Northeast National Marine Sanctuaries with Jean-Michel Cousteau*, visits sanctuaries off the east coast of the United States and in the Great Lakes region. The other books in the series are: *Explore the Southeast National Marine Sanctuaries with Jean-Michel Cousteau*, *Explore the West Coast National Marine Sanctuaries with Jean-Michel Cousteau* and *Explore the Pacific Islands National Marine Sanctuaries with Jean-Michel Cousteau*.

Jean-Michel Cousteau.
Photo credit: Matthew Ferraro, Ocean Futures Society.

The first National Marine Sanctuary in the United States was established only three decades ago, while Yellowstone, the oldest of America's National Parks, was created in 1872. By comparison to parks, these natural marine jewels were damaged upon arrival. Only small portions remain pristine. For many, their designations arose amidst threats to one or a number of aspects to their survival. Like terrestrial parks, these are special habitats, managed zones for the recovery of critical species like humpback whales or juvenile rockfish but, most importantly, they attempt to preserve the integrity of the web of life.

Ironically, we discovered that managing these resources for sustainability was in truth an exercise in managing ourselves. And that's not, as we're still learning, an easy job. At each destination we were privileged witnesses to the real-time drama of marine conservation playing out across the United States. At the heart of it all, we found a powerful paradigm shift happening in environmentalism. Fishermen, environmentalists and scientists from opposite sides of the aisle were sitting down together with rolled-up sleeves, poring through scientific research, debating the merits of reserves and restoration, and coming to terms with this new definition of sanctuary. "These are," as Dan Basta, Director of the National Marine Sanctuary System, reminded us, "still works in progress."

About National Marine Sanctuaries

The Office of National Marine Sanctuaries, part of the National Oceanic and Atmospheric Administration, manages a national system of underwater-protected areas. The National Marine Sanctuary Act (created in 1972) authorizes the Secretary of Commerce to designate specific areas as National Marine Sanctuaries to promote comprehensive management of their special ecological, historical, recreational, and aesthetic resources. The Office of National Marine Sanctuaries currently manages thirteen National Marine Sanctuaries and one Marine National Monument established in areas where the natural or cultural resources are so significant that they warrant special status and protection.

On January 6, 2009, President George W. Bush established three additional marine national monuments, which were placed into the Pacific Reefs National Wildlife Refuge Complex. The three new marine national monuments are the Pacific Remote Islands Marine National Monument, Marianas Trench Marine National Monument, and the Rose Atoll Marine National Monument. Because Jean-Michel Cousteau and his Ocean Futures Society team have not yet dived in these three remote areas, they are not included in this series. Furthermore, these new monuments are managed by the US Fish and Wildlife Service, and not by the National Oceanic and Atmospheric Administration, the managing agency of the National Marine Sanctuaries and one Marine National Monument featured here.

The Office of National Marine Sanctuaries works cooperatively with the public and federal, state, and local officials to promote conservation while allowing compatible commercial and recreational activities in the Sanctuaries. Increasing public awareness of our marine heritage, scientific research, monitoring, exploration, educational programs, and outreach are just a few of the ways the Office of National Marine Sanctuaries fulfills its mission to the American people. The primary objective of a sanctuary is to protect its natural and cultural features while allowing people to use and enjoy the ocean in a sustainable way. Sanctuary waters provide a secure habitat for species close to extinction and protect historically significant shipwrecks and artifacts. Sanctuaries serve as natural classrooms and laboratories for schoolchildren and researchers alike to promote understanding and stewardship of our oceans. They often are cherished recreational spots for sport fishing and diving and support commercial industries such as tourism, fishing and kelp harvesting.

Today (2007), only 0.01 percent of the world's oceans are effectively protected, a comparatively small measure, and one most scientists are quick to caution isn't a panacea for all the ocean's troubles. But it's enough nonetheless, to keep some fisheries managers and fishermen hopeful about sustainably harvesting fish from the sea. In the face of collapsing fisheries, "They may help some exploited species recover and keep others from going entirely extinct," according to Daniel Pauly, a researcher with the Fisheries Center at the University of British Columbia. He postulates that marine protected areas "should help prevent this, just like forests and other natural terrestrial habitats have enabled the survival of wildlife species, which agriculture would have otherwise rendered extinct."

The mission of NOAA's National Marine Sanctuaries is to serve as the trustee for the nation's system of marine protected areas, to conserve, protect, and enhance their biodiversity, ecological integrity and cultural legacy. The National Marine Sanctuary System consists of more than 150,000 square miles (390,000 km²) of marine and Great Lakes waters located from Washington State to the Florida Keys; from Lake Huron to American Samoa. Within these protected waters, giant humpback whales breed and calve their young, temperate reefs flourish, and shipwrecks tell stories of our maritime history. Today, our marine sanctuary system encompasses deep ocean gardens, nearshore coral reefs, whale migration corridors, deep sea canyons, and even underwater archeological sites. The sites range in size from one-quarter square mile (0.6 km²) in Fagatele Bay, American Samoa to more than 135,000 square miles (350,000 km²) in the Northwestern Hawaiian Islands, one of the largest marine protected areas in the world. Each sanctuary site is a unique place needing special protections. Natural classrooms, cherished recreational spots, and valuable commercial industries—marine sanctuaries represent many things to many people.

The National Marine Sanctuaries' Northeast Region

Over thirty years ago, Congress passed the Marine Protection, Research and Sanctuaries Act of 1972. Three years later, in 1975, the wreck site of the USS *Monitor* became the nation's first national marine sanctuary. From the first to the newest sanctuary, the Northeast regional office protects not only the USS *Monitor* but also natural and cultural resources at Stellwagen Bank, and a vast collection of Great Lakes wrecks in Thunder Bay, the nation's newest and only freshwater sanctuary, created solely to protect underwater cultural resources.

Sanctuaries often face daunting challenges, like the crowded shipping lanes and dense fishing gear deployments that threaten endangered marine mammals feeding in the Stellwagen Bank area. Stellwagen Bank is considered one of the top whale watching sites in the world. Stellwagen Bank is also home to the wreck of the coastal steam ship, the *Portland,* which was listed on the National Register of Historic Places in January 2005.

This book will introduce readers to the **Thunder Bay**, **Stellwagen Bank**, and *Monitor* sanctuaries.

Northeast, Mid-Atlantic and Great Lakes National Marine Sanctuary Regional Office:
10 Ocean Science Circle
Savannah, GA 31411
Telephone: 912-598-2345

Thunder Bay

About Thunder Bay National Marine Sanctuary

Located in northwestern Lake Huron, Thunder Bay is adjacent to one of the most treacherous stretches of water within the Great Lakes system. Unpredictable weather, murky fog banks, sudden gales, and rocky shoals earned the area the name "Shipwreck Alley." Today, the 448-square-mile (1160-square-kilometer) Thunder Bay National Marine Sanctuary protects one of America's best-preserved and nationally-significant collections of shipwrecks. Fire, ice, collisions, and storms have claimed many vessels in and around Thunder Bay. To date, there are 45 known historic shipwrecks in the Sanctuary's current boundaries and archival research suggests that another 38 are yet to be found. Just outside the Sanctuary boundaries in the two counties north and south of Alpena there are 39 known shipwrecks and the potential to locate 60 more.

The remains of the steamer W.P. Thew lie in 84 feet of water east of Thunder Bay Island. One of the highlights of the dive on this ship is exploring the open engine and boiler of the steamer. The W.P. Thew is buoyed by the Sanctuary annually. Photo credit: NOAA, Thunder Bay National Marine Sanctuary.

Thunder Bay National Marine Sanctuary was designated by the National Oceanic and Atmospheric Administration (NOAA) on October 7, 2000. It is jointly managed by NOAA and the State of Michigan to protect and interpret a nationally significant collection of shipwrecks and other maritime heritage resources. The Michigan Historical Center represents the state in managing the Sanctuary. Thunder Bay is the only freshwater national marine sanctuary in the U.S.

Thunder Bay is a kind of watery museum along the coast of Michigan's Lower Peninsula, where some 200 shipwrecks of nearly every type of vessel that ever traversed the inland seas are preserved in Lake Huron's frigid depths. Wrecks in varying states of ruin lie in only 12 feet (3.5 meters) of water, or as deep as 200 feet (61 meters). Some vessels are relatively intact, while only the remnants of boilers, engines, rudders, windlasses, and anchors remain of others.

The intact starboard side of the bow of the Van Valkenburg *shows stark contrast when compared to its damaged port side. The stern of the schooner* Lucinda Van Valkenburg *rests in 60 feet of water Northeast of Thunder Bay Island. The ship was lost in 1887 after a 25 year career sailing on the Great Lakes. This wreck is buoyed by the Sanctuary every summer. Photo credit: NOAA, Thunder Bay National Marine Sanctuary.*

Why a National Marine Sanctuary?

For over 12,000 years, people have traveled on the Great Lakes. From Native American dugout canoes to wooden sailing craft and steel freighters, thousands of ships have made millions of voyages across the Great Lakes. The last 150 years have been particularly dynamic, transforming the region into one of the world's busiest waterways. Yet, increased risk often shadows such extraordinary growth. Nearly 200 pioneer steamboats, majestic schooners, and huge steel freighters wrecked near Thunder Bay alone. Although the sheer number of shipwrecks is impressive, it is the range of vessel types located in the Sanctuary that makes the collection nationally significant. From an 1844 sidewheel steamer to a modern 500-foot (152-meter) long German freighter, the shipwrecks of Thunder Bay represent a microcosm of maritime commerce and travel on the Great Lakes.

By the 1850s, Lake Huron's Thunder Bay was a hub of trade and commerce and the port of Alpena was a boomtown, growing tenfold in a little over a dozen years. Settlers were drawn from New York, New England, Canada, and as far away as Sweden and Norway, all seeking fortunes in a land that promised the adventurous what seemed like unlimited natural resources—free for the taking. The European demand for furs fueled deeper exploration of the Great Lakes and their tributaries. At the turn of the nineteenth century, an indispensable means of transportation was still the canoe, stable and able to portage around obstacles. Gradually small sloop-rigged sailboats became more common for coastal travel and, as the supply of animals for pelts dwindled and more attention turned towards fishing, the sloop became the vessel utilized by commercial fleets.

The Great Lakes fisheries, however, were soon impacted by an expanding lumber industry. Floating logs tore up river bottoms, and waste cuttings and decaying sawdust depleted available oxygen. Swamps were drained, shorelines filled in and navigation channels were dredged, all degrading the nearshore aquatic habitat even further. By 1886, it was reported that fish stocks had decreased by as much as two-thirds.

Timber replaced fisheries as the new economy and steam-powered vessels became more common on the lakes, carrying passengers and freight. The growing cities of the Midwest—Cleveland, Buffalo, Toronto, Milwaukee, and Detroit—were importing timber as quickly as it could be felled.

The bow of the two-masted schooner EB Allen, *sunk in 1871, now lies within the Thunder Bay National Marine Sanctuary. Photo credit: NOAA, Thunder Bay National Marine Sanctuary.*

The converted barkentine Ogarita *sank when its cargo of coal caught fire while she was in tow of a steamship in 1905. The ship's keelson still stands strong through the center of the shipwreck and its sides are partially exposed rising out of the sand. The* Ogarita *is buoyed by the Sanctuary and lies in 30 feet of water north of Thunder Bay Island. Photo credit: NOAA, Thunder Bay National Marine Sanctuary.*

Today, the Sanctuary's shipwrecks capture dramatic moments from centuries that transformed America. As a collection, they illuminate an era of enormous growth and remind us of risks taken and tragedies endured. Lake Huron's cold, fresh water ensures that Thunder Bay's shipwrecks are among the best preserved in the world. Many sites have remained virtually unchanged for over 150 years. With masts still standing, deck hardware in place, and the crews' personal possessions often surviving, sites located in deeper waters are true time capsules. Other shipwrecks lay well-preserved but broken up in shallower waters. Readily accessible by kayakers, snorkelers, and divers of all abilities, these sites often provide Sanctuary users with their first shipwreck experience.

The wreck of the Maid of the Mist *lies in very shallow waters. Photo credit: Donald Tipton.*

Thunder Bay's shipwrecks are magnificent, yet vulnerable. Natural processes and human impacts threaten the long-term sustainability of our underwater maritime heritage. Ice, waves, and aquatic invasive species such as zebra and quagga mussels could potentially harm maritime heritage resources. Through research, education, and community involvement, the Sanctuary works to protect our nation's historic shipwrecks for future generations. Protecting Thunder Bay's underwater treasures is a responsibility shared by the Sanctuary, its many partners, and the public.

Before Thunder Bay's designation as the nation's thirteenth national marine sanctuary in 2000, the state of Michigan created the Thunder Bay Underwater Preserve, a 290-square-mile (751-square-kilometer) area designated in 1981 as the first of eleven preserves authorized by Michigan's "Bottomlands Act." The 448-square-mile (1160-square-kilometer) area of Lake Huron is now both a national marine sanctuary and a state underwater preserve.

Research divers in Thunder Bay. Photo credit: Steve Sellers.

Resources within the Thunder Bay National Marine Sanctuary

Northeastern Michigan's maritime landscape includes the hundreds of shipwrecks located on Lake Huron bottomlands. It also encompasses all of the cultural and natural features related to maritime heritage. Lifesaving stations, lighthouses, historic boats and ships, commercial fishing camps, docks, and working ports are among the more obvious historic and archaeological features. Many features are less visible and some remain unrecognized or unknown. Humans have used the waters of Thunder Bay and its shores for thousands of years. Geological and archaeological evidence suggests a high probability of prehistoric archaeological sites awaiting discovery. In addition to helping to protect and interpret individual sites, managing the Sanctuary as a maritime cultural landscape reveals a broad his-

Launched in 1891, the Grecian *symbolizes an era of unprecedented industrial growth and dramatic changes in technology. Newspapers heralded the* Grecian *and her five sister ships as "fast steel flyers." A marvel of efficiency for her time, the* Grecian *made an impressive 35 trips and carried 93,000 tons of iron ore in 1896 - all for just 23 cents per mile in fuel. Image credit: Thunder Bay Sanctuary Research Collection.*

torical canvas that can encompass many different perspectives to foster an interconnected understanding of the maritime past. The maritime cultural landscape allows Thunder Bay's maritime heritage to continue to unfold as new discoveries are made and encourages an increasingly diverse public to find shared meaning in this nationally and internationally significant place.

Key wrecks within the Sanctuary

We were on our way to dive in the Great Lakes when we were offered a mission: survey two newly discovered wrecks on the bottom of icy Lake Huron and collect evidence that would help corroborate accounts of a mysterious accident that had happened over a century ago.

Jean-Michel Cousteau on the Pride of Michigan, *the support vessel for Ocean Futures' filming operations on Lake Huron. Photo credit: Carrie Vonderhaar, Ocean Futures Society.*

Thunder Bay Island lighthouse was a landmark that would bring a lot of ships close together, but the increase in shipping traffic also increased the risk of collisions. Two sailing ships, the Defiance *and the* John J. Audubon, *were the victims of just such a set of circumstances; but the details of the catastrophe have remained sketchy.*

It was too intriguing of an opportunity for us to pass up. Our closed-circuit rebreathers would allow us to spend more time at the 180 to 200 foot (55 to 61 meter) depths than scuba, time we'd need to make measurements and film what remained of the structures laying on the lake floor.

The Ocean Futures team films the wreck of the John J. Audubon.
Photo credit: Carrie Vonderhaar, Ocean Futures Society.

Defiance

Classification: Wooden Two-Masted Schooner
Depth: 150 feet (46 meters)
Wreck Length: 115 feet (35 meters)
Beam: 26 feet (eight meters)
Built: 1848 by Capt. Roby at Perryburg, Ohio
Wrecked: October 20, 1854.
Description: At just after 1 o'clock in the morning the two-masted schooner *Defiance* was run into by the *J.J. Audubon* off Presque Isle. Both vessels were fatally injured and sank within a few miles of one another. *Defiance* is remarkably preserved with masts upright and little damage to the hull. The wreck was discovered in 1996.

The ninety-foot masts still stand on the Defiance. *Photo credit: NOAA, Thunder Bay National Marine Sanctuary.*

E.B. Allen[1]

Classification: Wooden Two-Masted Schooner
Depth: 100 feet (30.5 meters)
Wreck Length: 134 feet (41 meters)
Beam: 26 feet (eight meters)
Launched: 1864 by H.C. Piersons at Ogdensburg, New York
Wrecked: November 20, 1871
Description: On its last voyage, the *E.B. Allen* was bound for Buffalo, New York, carrying a cargo of grain. When it was about two miles (three kilometers) southeast of Thunder Bay Island, it met the bark *Newsboy* in heavy fog. The two ships collided, and the *Newsboy* tore a large hole in the *Allen's* portside. As the ship began to sink, the *Allen's* crew was removed and taken on board the other vessel. Today, the *E.B. Allen* sits on an even keel, with its hull largely intact. Although the masts are broken and most of the decking is gone, the windlass, anchor chains, and rudder are still in place.

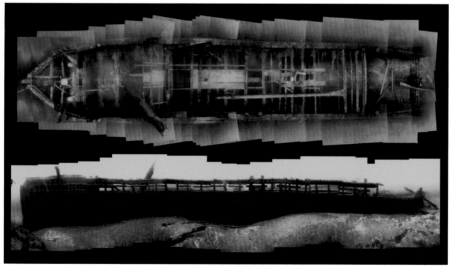

Photomosaics of the E.B. Allen. *Image credit: NOAA, Thunder Bay National Marine Sanctuary.*

---

1   There is a seasonal mooring buoy at this wreck. See http://thunderbay.noaa.gov/wreck_coordinates.html for coordinates.

F.T. Barney

Classification: Two-Masted Schooner
Depth: 160 feet (49 meters)
Wreck Length: 126 feet (38 meters)
Beam: 26 feet (eight meters)
Built: 1856 by W. Cheney at Vermillion, Ohio
Wrecked: October 23, 1868
Description: En route from Cleveland to Milwaukee, *F.T. Barney* was run into by the schooner *T.J. Bronson*. The ship sank in less than two minutes in very deep water with a cargo of coal. No lives were lost. The wreck is one of the most complete of its kind with masts and deck equipment still in place. The wreck was discovered in 1987.

A close up view of the bow of the schooner FT Barney *lying intact on the bottom of Lake Huron.*
Photo credit: NOAA, Thunder Bay National Marine Sanctuary.

Ships that wreck in shallow water tend to break apart due to the force of wind, waves, and ice. Many wrecks dot the shoreline of Thunder Bay, providing great opportunities for snorkeling, kayaking, and recreational diving. Pictured here is the schooner American Union. *These wrecks make for great snorkel adventures. Photo credit: NOAA Office of Ocean Exploration and Research.*

American Union

Classification: 3-Masted Schooner
Depth: 10 feet (three meters)
Wreck Length: 185 feet (56 meters)
Beam: 25 feet (7.6 meters)
Built: 1862 by Ira Lafrinier at Cleveland, Ohio
Wrecked: May 6, 1894
Description: Larger than the typical schooner of its time, *American Union's* deep draft got it in trouble more than once. When rounding Presque Isle in a heavy sea the ship ran up on the rocks at Thompson's Harbor and quickly broke apart. Its remains are now scattered and flattened on the lake bottom but are easily viewable to kayakers and snorkelers.

B.W. Blanchard

Classification: Steam Barge
Depth: 9 feet (2.7 meters)
Wreck Length: 221 feet (67 meters)
Beam: 32.4 feet (10 meters)
Built: 1870 by Quayle and Martin at Cleveland, Ohio
Wrecked: November 29, 1904
Description: The *B.W. Blanchard* and its consort schooner barges *John T. Johnson* and *John Kilderhouse* ran aground together on North Point Reef during a blinding snowstorm. The *Kilderhouse* was later pulled off the rocks but *Blanchard* and *Johnson* stuck fast and soon went to pieces. Their remains are now intermixed in very shallow water easily accessible to kayakers and snorkelers.

Historic image (top) and remains (next page) of the B.W. Blanchard. *Photo credits: Thunder Bay Sanctuary Research Collection (top) and NOAA, Thunder Bay National Marine Sanctuary (next page).*

Florida

Classification: Package Freighter
Depth: 206 Feet (63 meters)
Wreck Length: 270 feet (82 meters)
Beam: 40 feet (12 meters)
Built: 1889 by Robert Mills at Buffalo, New York
Wrecked: May 21, 1897
Description: During a dense fog the steamer *Florida* was sunk by collision with the steamer *George W. Roby* off Middle Island. The ship went down in deep water and was nearly cut in half by the collision. *Florida* sits upright on the lake bottom and still contains much of its package freight. The wreck was located in 1994.

NOAA archaeologists document the damaged stern of the wooden freighter SS Florida. *Photo credit: NOAA, Thunder Bay National Marine Sanctuary.*

Wreck of the side-wheel steamer New Orleans. *Photo credit: NOAA, Thunder Bay National Marine Sanctuary.*

New Orleans[2]

Classification: Wooden Side Wheel Steamboat
Depth: 15 feet (4.5 meters)
Wreck Length: 130 feet (40 meters)
Beam: 27 feet (eight meters)
Launched: 1838 by B.F. Goodsell at Detroit, Michigan
Wrecked: June 14, 1849
Description: The propellers *William R. Linn* and *New Orleans* tried to pass each other on the same path during a fog. The ships collided and the *New Orleans*, getting the worst of it, sank in a few moments after receiving the deathblow. The wreck, still loaded with coal, is broken nearly in two but is considerably intact with mast stumps and deck equipment still in place.

---

2   There is a seasonal mooring buoy at this wreck. See http://thunderbay.noaa.gov/wreck_coordinates.html for coordinates.

Grecian[3]

Classification: Steel Bulk Freighter
Depth: 100 feet (30.5 meters); Stern Deck at 75 feet (23 meters)
Wreck Length: 296 feet (90 meters)
Beam: 40 feet (12 meters)
Launched: 1891 by Globe Iron Works at Cleveland, Ohio
Wrecked: June 15, 1906
Description: One June 7, 1906 the *Grecian* struck a rock and sank in shallow water at Detour Village in the St. Mary's River. The ship was later refloated and taken in tow by the steamer *Sir Henry Bessemer*, en route to Detroit for repairs. Unexpectedly, it filled with water and sank near Thunder Bay Island. Its crew escaped in lifeboats. Today the *Grecian's* bow and stern lie intact, while the midships portion has collapsed. The engine, boiler, portions of the propeller and deck machinery are all in place. There is also a steel canalon (salvage lifting device) lying off the vessel's stern from a 1909 salvage attempt.

The nearly intact stern of the steel steamer Grecian *lies in 95 feet of water. This part of the wreck holds the ship's tiller, engine and boiler. The remains of a failed salvage attempt lie nearby on the port side at the stern. Photo credit: NOAA, Thunder Bay National Marine Sanctuary.*

---

3   There is a seasonal mooring buoy at this wreck. See http://thunderbay.noaa.gov/wreck_coordinates.html for coordinates.

Emerging Environmental Issues

Invasive species: Zebra and Quagga mussels

Introduced to the Great Lakes via the ballast tanks of trans-Atlantic cargo ships, quaggas are natives of the Black Sea and were first noticed in Lake Erie in 1989. Since then, both zebra and quagga mussels have clogged freshwater intake pipes, fouled ships, and ruined beaches. Presently (2007), quagga mussels are found in four of the five Great Lakes. They are colonizing deeper, colder regions where conditions are unfavorable to zebras, and are replacing zebras in shallow waters too.

Alien invaders—quagga mussels from the Black Sea—encrust the wooden hull of the Audubon. Photo credit: Carrie Vonderhaar, Ocean Futures Society

Where large populations of quagga and zebra mussels grow, the water tends to be very clear.

"That's fairly typical of what we see throughout the Great Lakes." Tom[4] *goes on to explain, "Adult mussels can filter about a liter (1 quart) of water a day . . . multiply that by the number of mussels you see here and they can turn the water over very rapidly."*

"Well, a lot of people would say that's great," suggests Fabien.[5]

"Well, it's not, unfortunately," Tom replies. "Particles in the water are mostly phytoplankton and basically the mussels are filtering out food material that is used by other organisms in the food chain leading up to fish...a lot of species in the Great Lakes are now declining...becoming rare because of this explosion of mussels."

4　Tom Nalepa is a research biologist with NOAA's Great Lakes Environmental Research Lab
5　Fabien Cousteau

"You know, because the water's so clear, it makes the ships that are at the bottom look like they were sailing on kind of a moonscape," reflects Fabien. "But what really shocked me was the lack of life. I never saw a fish, not one. But I did see lots of quagga mussels encrusting a ship that just a few years ago had very few, if any on it. Although I was amongst team-mates, I felt very alone down there because there was no other life. It brings it so close to home, how very careful we need to be everyday because we do have a huge impact," he acknowledges to Tom. "And how very quickly we can erase life around us by our actions, whether intentional or not."

The shipwrecked John J. Audubon, *constructed circa 1858, rests at the bottom of Lake Huron, Michigan. Photo credit: Carrie Vonderhaar, Ocean Futures Society*

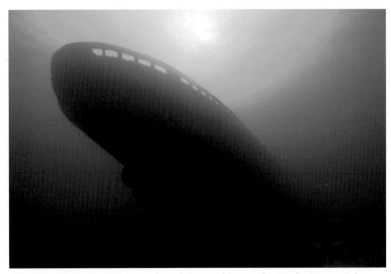

The stern of the Grecian, *seen from below. Photo credit: Becky Kagan Schott, Woods Hole Oceanographic Institution.*

In 2000, Nalepa says, his survey showed an average of 899 zebra mussels per square meter (84 mussels per square foot) of lake bottom at 160 sites in Lake Michigan. Within just five years, however, quaggas had reached 7,790 mussels per square meter (728 mussels per square foot), far out-pacing the earlier invaders. As the invasion of foreign mussels advances, native mussels are being pushed out of existence, and along with them, a glacial relic, a tiny shrimp-like amphipod called Diporeia is also vanishing. Fish that feed on Diporeia "no longer have it as a food source." Other bizarre things are happening to fish. Before zebra mussels were found in Lake Michigan, the average seven-year-old whitefish weighed more than five pounds (2.3 kg). Eight years later, after the invasion, it weighs only 1.6 pounds (0.7 kg).

Invasive mussels surround the manufacturer's plate on the steam drum of the Montana. *Photo credit: NOAA, Thunder Bay National Marine Sanctuary.*

Invasive species like the quagga are the second leading cause of extinction of native species after habitat loss. And solutions to fixing the problems don't come cheap. On average, it is estimated that nearly 300 billion dollars a year is spent globally on damage and pest control.

Research within the Sanctuary

Thunder Bay National Marine Sanctuary conducts, supports, promotes, and coordinates scientific research and monitoring of its maritime heritage resources to ensure their long-term protection. Archaeological and historical research conducted by the Sanctuary and its partners is fundamental to better understanding the region's historic shipwrecks. This knowledge is essential for addressing management issues and enhancing resource protection. Research priorities include:

- **Characterization of the Sanctuary's maritime heritage resources and landscape features:** This involves conducting historical and archival research on potential maritime heritage resources and landscape features in and around the Sanctuary, conducting systematic remote sensing and visual surveys to locate and identify maritime heritage resources and landscape features in the Sanctuary, and establishing baseline data for long-term monitoring.

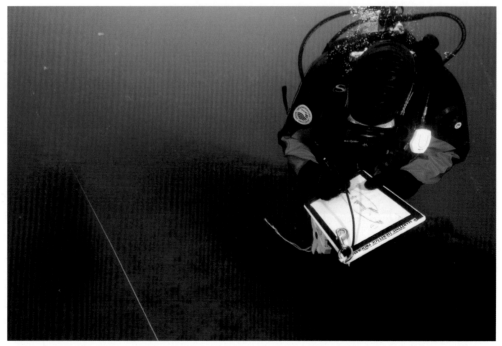

Research diver documenting information on a shipwreck in the Thunder Bay National Marine Sanctuary. Photo credit: NOAA, Thunder Bay National Marine Sanctuary.

- **Multi-disciplinary research:** The Sanctuary is developing partnerships with multi-disciplinary researchers and organizations to study Great Lakes ecology including climate change, invasive species, lake biology, geology, and water quality. The Sanctuary is working with university and NOAA scientists to develop long term monitoring programs to better understand how the chemical, biological, and physical conditions found around Thunder Bay's shipwrecks are affecting the corrosion and deterioration of these irreplaceable archaeological sites.

- **Artificial reef restoration:** The Michigan Department of Environmental Quality is restoring 12 artificial reefs in Lake Huron's Thunder Bay to allow recovery of reef habitat lost by the past deposition of cement kiln dust along the shoreline and lake bottom. This project will allow further recovery of lake trout populations in the area.

Students from Sanborn Elementary School's Thunder Bay River Watershed Project worked with divers from the Sanctuary field team to set up a zebra mussel experiment near the shipwreck Oscar T. Flint, *took water samples, and also launched their remotely operated vehicles from the deck of R/V* Storm. *Photo credit: NOAA, Thunder Bay National Marine Sanctuary.*

Research Assets

R/V *STORM*

The 50-foot (15-meter) R/V *Storm* is operated by the NOAA Great Lakes Environmental Research Lab and is dedicated to supporting the marine activities of the Thunder Bay National Marine Sanctuary. The RV *Storm* is a "Green Ship" in NOAA's Great Lakes fleet. The B100 fuel is produced from soy bean oil and reduces emissions by more than 70 percent. The engine oil, lubricants and hydraulic oils are manufactured from a variety of vegetable oils. These bio materials are sustainable and far less toxic than conventional petroleum oils. All ship-board systems and practices were engineered for efficiency and minimal environmental impact.

Visiting the Sanctuary

Note: In the last section of the book, "When You Visit the Sanctuaries," is detailed information about resources found within each sanctuary to help visitors have an enjoyable and productive visit.

VISITOR'S CENTER
Great Lakes Maritime Heritage Center
500 W. Fletcher Street
Alpena, MI 49707

Open year-round
Hours vary by season, but generally the Center is open Monday through Saturday in winter months, and Monday through Sunday in the summer. Because times may change, visitors should check the Sanctuary website before planning a visit.[6]
Admission: Free
Telephone: 989-356-8805

The Great Lakes Maritime Heritage Center is a visitor center for the Thunder Bay National Marine Sanctuary, featuring exciting exhibits for all ages. The center's main hall includes a full-size replica wooden Great Lakes schooner and shipwreck where visitors can walk the decks, feel a Great Lakes storm, and touch the massive timbers of the boat resting on the lake bottom...without getting wet.

---

6   http://thunderbay.noaa.gov/maritime/glmhc.html

The cardboard boat race is one of the highlights of the Thunder Bay National Marine Sanctuary's annual Maritime Festival. Thousands of visitors celebrate the region's maritime heritage at this free July event each year. Photo credit: NOAA, Thunder Bay National Marine Sanctuary.

The Great Lakes Maritime Heritage Center features:

- 9,000 square feet (836 square meters) of immersive exhibits
- 93-seat theater showing films daily
- Archaeological conservation lab and shipwreck artifact gallery
- Innovative education space for special programs, meetings, and events
- Scientific research facilities, including a dive operations center
- Community boat-building center
- Outdoor access to the Great Lakes Maritime Heritage Trail and open-air picnic grounds
- Maritime Heritage Center Gift Shop

The Center is Gold LEED certified[7] and the Sanctuary's "green story" is told throughout the exhibits.

Thunder Bay National Marine Sanctuary's visitor center, the Great Lakes Maritime Heritage Center. Photo credit: NOAA, Thunder Bay National Marine Sanctuary.

---

7   LEED certification provides independent, third-party verification that a building, home or community was designed and built using strategies aimed at achieving high performance in key areas of human and environmental health: sustainable site development, water savings, energy efficiency, materials selection and indoor environmental quality. Levels of certification are (from lowest to highest) certified, silver, gold and platinum.

Thunder Bay National Marine Sanctuary Office
The Sanctuary office is adjacent to the Great Lakes Maritime Heritage Center at
500 W. Fletcher Street
Alpena, Michigan 49707
Telephone: 989-356-8805

Visitors to the Thunder Bay National Marine Sanctuary can experience everything from fantastic recreational diving to exciting kayaking and boating. Divers at Thunder Bay are able to explore numerous shipwrecks and thereby discover a vast collection of maritime stories. From wooden schooners to early steel-hulled steamers, divers are able to see first-hand the hidden treasures of America's past. Sanctuary visitors who prefer to stay above the water can view the water's surface and natural surroundings by sailing, boating, kayaking or canoeing. Another option lies with staying on dry land and fishing, bird watching, or learning about the Great Lakes maritime history by visiting local museums or lighthouses.

ECO-TOURS
Glass-bottom boat tours to visit shipwrecks in Thunder Bay are available.

The 65-foot glass bottom boat Lady Michigan offers tours of some of the shipwrecks in the Sanctuary. Photo credit: NOAA, Thunder Bay National Marine Sanctuary.

Wrecks lying in shallow water are clearly visible through the glass bottom boat's viewing windows.
Photo credit: NOAA, Thunder Bay National Marine Sanctuary.

BOATING

The Sanctuary protects a large collection of shipwrecks that offer incredible canoeing and kayaking opportunities. A number of convenient access points along the shores of Lake Huron make Thunder Bay shipwreck paddling fun and feasible recreation. Excursions can vary from a one-hour paddle to multi-day trips along the coast.

Many shipwrecks in the Sanctuary are in very shallow water and can be easily observed from a kayak.
Photo credit: NOAA, Thunder Bay National Marine Sanctuary.

FISHING

A Michigan fishing license is required for residents and visitors who are 17 years old or older.[8]

---

8   www.michigan.gov/dnr

DIVING/SNORKELING

Access to Sanctuary shipwrecks is not restricted. The range of depth of the shipwrecks appeals to a variety of diver skill levels and also promises recreational opportunities for non-divers. The shallower wrecks can be viewed by snorkelers, kayakers, and boaters. To facilitate recreational access, the Sanctuary invests in mooring buoys designed to improve safety and access to resources, while reducing visitor impacts. These mooring buoys are deployed during summer months.

Mooring buoy deployment. Photo credit: NOAA, Thunder Bay National Marine Sanctuary.

Located just off the coast of Alpena, Michigan, the known shipwrecks in Thunder Bay[9] rest in waters ranging from 12 to 180 feet (3.6 to 55 meters) deep. Among them are wooden schooners, barks, brigs, steamers, barges, tugboats, steel-hulled steamers and freighters — a veritable catalogue of American maritime history spanning almost 200 years, preserved in exceptional condition by the cold, fresh waters of Lake Huron. Visibility is generally excellent, with many days well over 100 feet (30.5 meters). The maximum surface temperature by August reaches the mid-70°Fs (about 24°C), though depths greater than 45 feet (13.7 meters) stay in the mid-50°F s (about 13°C), and drop to the 30°Fs (about 1.5°C) in technical diving ranges. Dive season starts around Memorial Day and extends through mid-October.

A diver investigates the wheel from the schooner FT Barney.
Photo credit: NOAA, Thunder Bay National Marine Sanctuary.

---

9   http://thunderbay.noaa.gov/shipwrecks/vesseldata.html

Quick Facts

- Visibility: 20 – 100 feet (6 – 30.5 meters)
- 30° – 65° F (-1°–18°C)
- Beginner to advanced divers
- May–August

Ocean Futures Society's Matthew Ferraro flies the Explorer's Club flag on the mast of the Defiance.
Photo credit: Chuck Davis, Ocean Futures Society (high definition video frame grab.)

Stellwagen Bank

About Gerry E. Studds Stellwagen Bank National Marine Sanctuary

STELLWAGEN BANK National Marine Sanctuary lies in the heart of New England's fishing grounds, roughly 25 miles (40 kilometers) east of Boston, between Cape Cod and Gloucester. It can only be distinguished by an oblique border on nautical charts marking a plateau that rises from the surrounding sea floor to within 65 feet (20 meters) of the surface. The jutting bathymetry of the underwater bank creates an island of upwelling that is one of the most productive regions in the northwestern Atlantic and is why hundreds of species, from pelagic fish to seabirds and large marine mammals, rely on Stellwagen Bank for food.

Two humpback whales and sea birds actively feed in the waters of Stellwagen Bank National Marine Sanctuary. Credit: Stellwagen Bank National Marine Sanctuary. Photo taken under NOAA Fisheries Permit #605-1904.

In the southwest corner of the Gulf of Maine is Massachusetts Bay. The bay's most prominent submerged feature is the kidney-shaped plateau called Stellwagen Bank, which lies at the bay's eastern edge. Stellwagen Bank is a shallow, primarily sandy feature, curving in a southeast to northwest direction for 19 miles (30.6 kilometers). It is roughly six miles (10 kilometers) across at its widest point at the southern end. Water depths over and around the bank range from 65 feet (20 meters) on the southwest corner to about 600 feet (183 meters) in deep passages to the northeast. Massachusetts Basin on the western side of the Sanctuary levels off at about 300 feet (91 meters) in depth, while the top of the bank averages about 100 to 120 feet (30.5 to 36.6 meters).

The Boston skyline peeks out over the horizon behind Boston light. Stellwagen Bank National Marine Sanctuary lies to the east. Photo credit: Anne Smrcina, NOAA/ Stellwagen Bank National Marine Sanctuary.

Stellwagen Bank is the centerpiece of Stellwagen Bank National Marine Sanctuary, which encompasses a total of 842 square miles (2181 square kilometers). The Sanctuary boundary is somewhat rectangular, stretching from three miles southeast of Cape Ann to three miles north of Cape Cod. The Sanctuary is about 25 miles (40 kilometers) east of Boston, and lies totally within federal waters. It encompasses all of Stellwagen and Tillies Banks, and the southern portion of Jeffreys Ledge. From the Sanctuary's Scituate-based headquarters, the distance is approximately 11 miles (18 kilometers).

Located at the mouth of Massachusetts Bay, Stellwagen Bank National Marine Sanctuary sits astride the historic shipping lanes and fishing grounds for such ports as Boston, Gloucester, Plymouth, Salem, and Provincetown. These ports have been centers of maritime activity in New England for hundreds of years. Over time accidents have occurred and ships have sunk leaving virtual time capsules on the seafloor. As a result, the Sanctuary has become a repository of maritime heritage resources, with shipwrecks serving as discrete windows into specific moments of our sea-going past.

Stellwagen Bank was named for the person who first mapped it in its entirety. Knowledge of shallow areas at the mouth of Massachusetts Bay had been around for many centuries. In fact, maps from the early 1700s showed an area called Barren Bank at what is now known as the southwest corner of the bank. Middle Bank (covering a good portion of Stellwagen Bank) was drawn on several 19th century maps. In 1854, Henry S. Stellwagen, a lieutenant of the US Navy on loan to the Coast Survey, was sent to Massachusetts with the task of mapping potential lighthouse positions. In the course of his work, he realized he had discovered a feature not represented on any official maps. Over the course of several months in 1854, he mapped the bank and the surrounding seafloor. The following year the U.S. government released a new map detailing this feature. The U.S. Coast Survey, recognizing the importance of the find and the work of Henry Stellwagen, named the geological feature after the man who documented the underwater feature.

Ocean Futures Society's vessel, the Manfish, *survives a nasty storm in Massachusetts Bay. Photo credit: Carrie Vonderhaar, Ocean Futures Society.*

The hull of the fishing vessel Josephine Marie *is full of life. Photo credit: Matthew Lawrence, NOAA/Stellwagen Bank National Marine Sanctuary.*

In 1854-1855 Henry Stellwagen mapped the bank that is now named after him.
Photo credit: Naval Historical Center.

Why a National Marine Sanctuary?

For centuries, Stellwagen Bank has proved to be a rich and productive fishing ground, particularly for groundfish species like cod, haddock and flounder. Fishermen have also been able to catch Atlantic bluefin tuna, large sharks, and schools of herring. During the second half of the 20th century, the area gained fame as a whale watching destination.

Schools of Atlantic bluefin tuna cruise through the Gulf of Maine and sanctuary waters during their annual migration up the eastern seaboard. Photo credit: Gregory Skomal, Mass. Division of Marine Fisheries.

Two distinct peak productivity periods produce a complex system of habitats along the seafloor and throughout the water column. These communities support benthic and pelagic species by providing cover and anchoring locations for invertebrates; they also provide feeding and nursery grounds for more than 22 species of marine mammals including the endangered humpback, North Atlantic right, sei, and fin whales. The area supports foraging activity by diverse seabird species, dominated by gannets, fulmars, shearwaters, storm petrels, cormorants, phalaropes, alcids, gulls, jaegers, and terns. Fish and invertebrate populations subject to seasonal and migration shifts include both demersal and pelagic species, such as bluefin tuna, herring, cod, flounders, lobster, and scallops. Leatherback, loggerhead and Kemp's ridley sea turtles (endangered species) use the area for feeding.

Birds following a fishing boat at Stellwagen Bank.
Photo credit: Stellwagen Bank National Marine Sanctuary.

Data strongly suggest the presence of more than 200 shipwreck sites within the Sanctuary. One important site that has already been investigated is the historically significant wreck of the steamship *Portland* which sank in 1898 during a gale named after the ship. Vessel traffic is steady due to the fact that the major shipping lanes to Boston pass through the Sanctuary. The presence of whales and fish, in turn, attract vessels engaged in watching the former and catching the latter.

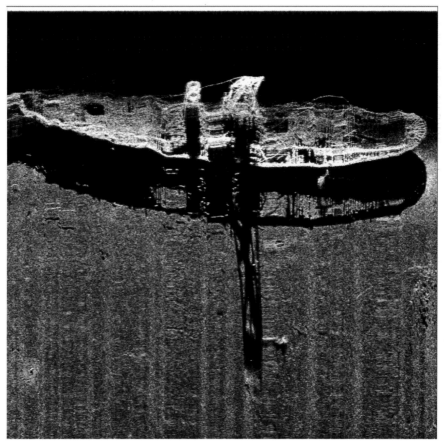

Side scan sonar image of the steamship Portland. Photo credit: L3 Communications/Klein Sonar Associates, Inc/Stellwagen Bank National Marine Sanctuary.

At the office of the Stellwagen Bank National Marine Sanctuary, conservation biologist Dave Wiley is working with marine archaeologists Dede Marx and Matt Lawrence to more closely investigate the life flourishing around the wreck of the Paul Palmer. Because of the high degree of biodiversity found there compared with areas around the Bank, the team is trying to piece together whether Stellwagen's historical resources — the wrecks known to rest on the seafloor and possibly hundreds more — might also be hotspots for recovering fish stocks.

The team films Jean-Michel exploring the Paul Palmer *wreck, a historic and ecological resource at Stellwagen Bank National Marine Sanctuary. Photo credit: Carrie Vonderhaar, Ocean Futures Society.*

Whaling, once an industry on Cape Cod, has been exchanged for whale watching. Truro and Provincetown were whaling towns in the 17th and 18th centuries – first with shore-based harvesting of stranded animals and then hunting from boats. By 1760, some 12 whaling ships called Provincetown their home. Now, whale watching companies depart from Provincetown and Barnstable on Cape Cod, while other companies base their operations in Plymouth, Boston, Gloucester and Newburyport.

Brightly colored buoys clutter the surface of the southwest corner (of Stellwagen Bank), evidence of a thriving lobster fishery that has operated here since the end of World War II. But these markers only hint at what lies hidden beneath the waves — a maze of hundreds of miles of lines and traps that stretch through the sea. With the collapse of New England's historic groundfisheries, lobstering has intensified and with it an increased risk to baleen whales that come here to feed. Humpbacks, fins, minkes, sei whales, and the critically endangered North Atlantic right whales all journey to Stellwagen Bank at different times of the year to forage on copepods and sand lance.

A humpback whale feeds near one of the many whale watching boats that visit Stellwagen Bank National Marine Sanctuary each year. Photo credit: Ari Friedlaender, Duke University. Stellwagen Bank National Marine Sanctuary file photo. Photo taken under NOAA Fisheries Permit #775-1875.

Advancements in technology have also altered the types of gear deployed at Stellwagen Bank. Single haul traps have been replaced with ground line trawls, where traps are strung together and deployed and hauled in series. The type of line used in the fishery has also changed; traditional, heavy sinking line has been replaced by floating polypropylene line that forms 20-foot (six-meter) high hoops that rise off the bottom between traps spaced 80 to 90 feet (24 to 27 meters) apart. Floating lines reduce the chance of the set snagging on rocks, which is good for fishermen, but has inadvertently made life infinitely more complicated for Stellwagen's whales.

Because of its long history of human use and its high natural productivity, Stellwagen Bank was first nominated for consideration as a national marine sanctuary in 1982. Stellwagen Bank National Marine Sanctuary was designated as the nation's 13th National Marine Sanctuary on November 4, 1992. In 1996, the Sanctuary was re-named as Gerry E. Studds Stellwagen Bank National Marine Sanctuary, to recognize retired Congressman Studds (D-MA) who was a staunch supporter of marine protection programs and was a leader in the effort to create and build the National Marine Sanctuary Program.

Lobster traps "fly" off the stern of a lobster boat during a set. Photo credit: Carrie Vonderhaar, Ocean Futures Society.

Capt. Frank Mirarchi and Ben Cowie-Haskell from the Sanctuary display a successful catch of derelict lobster traps from Stellwagen Bank National Marine Sanctuary. Photo credit: Dave Haley.

Resources within Stellwagen Bank National Marine Sanctuary

STELLWAGEN BANK

Stellwagen Bank is an underwater plateau at the mouth of Massachusetts Bay, formed by the same processes that formed outer Cape Cod. As the ice sheets of the last Great Ice Age retreated, they left behind sand, gravel and boulders. At one point in time (perhaps 12,000 years ago), Stellwagen Bank was above sea level, but as the glaciers continued to melt and sea level rose, the bank gradually submerged beneath the sea. Archaeological research may one day find prehistoric human, animal, or plant remains.

National Undersea Research Center--University of Connecticut

These holes in the mud of Stellwagen Basin may be the homes of American lobsters or Jonah crabs. Photo credit: Peter Auster and Paul Donaldson, Northeast Underwater Research, Technology and Education Center.

Stellwagen Bank's shallowest depths are at its southern end, which rises to within 65 feet of the surface. In this area, the sandy bottom is pockmarked with lobster holes. Moving north along the bank's top, the seafloor slopes to a relatively constant depth of 100 – 120 feet (30.5 – 36.5 meters). An area known as the Sponge Forest has cobble and scattered boulders that provide hard substrate for encrusting marine invertebrates such as the large finger sponges that gave inspiration for the location's name.

A finger sponge amidst the wooden remains and artifacts of an unidentified sailing vessel. Photo credit: NOAA/ Stellwagen Bank National Marine Sanctuary and Northeast Underwater Research Technology and Education Center.

In the sand and gravel areas on top of Stellwagen Bank live a variety of encrusting organisms such as sponges, tunicates, and anemones. Investigations reveal mussels, clams, scallops, moon snails, bryozoans, hydroids, sea stars and sand dollars. Fish life includes sculpins, skates, flounders, goosefish, and cod. Schools of dogfish, herring, pollock, and sand lance can be found on top of the bank.

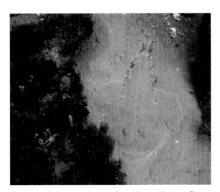

A goosefish lies camouflaged on the seafloor, near the Paul Palmer *wreck. Photo credit: Carrie Vonderhaar, Ocean Futures Society.*

On rocky ridges and boulder fields, as well as the remains of shipwrecks, a greater variety and density of encrusting invertebrates, in often spectacular color, are found. Wolffish and ocean pout can be found hiding between boulders and in crevices. Many of the fishes seen in the sand and gravel areas also frequent boulder and rocky areas.

Two ocean pout swim along the sandy seafloor near a sanctuary shipwreck. Photo credit: Matthew Lawrence, NOAA/Stellwagen Bank National Marine Sanctuary.

Bluefin tuna, and porbeagle, mako, white and blue sharks, as well as several varieties of gelatinous zooplankton can be found in the waters above the bank. Ocean sunfish and basking sharks feed on the jelly creatures, alongside humpback, minke, and fin whales. It is also possible to spot ocean sunfish and basking sharks. North Atlantic right whales travel through Stellwagen Bank's waters in the spring as they migrate from their winter calving grounds to their northern feeding areas.

North Atlantic right whales. Photo credit: NOAA.

JEFFREYS LEDGE

Jeffreys Ledge is a large glacial remnant, stretching 33 miles (53 kilometers) from offshore of Rockport, Massachusetts to Cape Elizabeth, Maine. On the northern edge of the Sanctuary, rocky ridges on the southern edge of Jeffreys Ledge rise to within 115 feet (35 meters) of the surface. The shallowest portion of the ledge is comprised of piled cobble and boulders. Anemones, stalked tunicates, and coralline algae reside on the rocks making for a colorful landscape when illuminated with a dive light. The ledge's piled boulders create a complex structure with many crevices for marine fishes like cusk and wolffish.

A cusk swims by a shipwreck in the Stellwagen Bank sanctuary. Photo credit: NOAA/Stellwagen Bank National Marine Sanctuary and Northeast Underwater Research, Technology and Education Center.

SANCTUARY HILL

A bedrock outcropping sits in the Sanctuary's northeast corner—Sanctuary Hill rises from 325 feet (99 meters) to 115 feet (35 meters) and is topped with solid granite and piled boulders. Like Jeffreys Ledge, the hill's hard substrate is home to a variety of invertebrates and fishes that live on and among the piled boulders. The Hill is 18 nautical miles (21 miles) offshore, and experiences very strong currents. Reportedly, blue and porbeagle sharks visit areas with steeply sloping topography like Sanctuary Hill.

Sharks such as this blue shark visit Stellwagen Bank to feed. Photo credit: Matthew Ferraro, Ocean Futures Society.

CULTURAL RESOURCES

Stellwagen Bank National Marine Sanctuary is home to numerous shipwrecks[1], reminders of this nation's maritime heritage. These shipwrecks are tangible connections to the past that allow people to study and better understand human history. Shipwrecks are nonrenewable gateways to the past and it is through the interpretation of these archaeological resources that the Sanctuary hopes to increase public enjoyment and appreciation of New England's maritime history and foster stewardship of America's maritime legacy. Six shipwreck sites comprised of seven vessels in the Sanctuary are listed on the National Register of Historic Places. These are the *Portland, Frank A. Palmer, Louise B. Crary, Paul Palmer, Joffre, Edna G* and a granite-carrying schooner.

---

1   http://stellwagen.noaa.gov/maritime/shipwrecks.html?

Steam escape pipe used to release pressure in the Portland's *boilers. Photo credit: NOAA/Stellwagen Bank National Marine Sanctuary, Northeast Underwater Research, Technology and Education Center and the Science Channel.*

The side paddle wheel steamship *Portland* was one of the largest and most palatial vessels afloat in New England during the 1890s. Built in 1889, the steamer ran between Portland, Maine and Boston until its loss with all hands in 1898. *Portland* now lies upright on a mud bottom with its wooden hull nearly intact from the keel up to the main deck level. The vessel's entire superstructure is missing with only the steam propulsion machinery protruding above deck level. Smaller cultural artifacts lie scattered inside and outside the hull providing a glimpse of the daily lifestyle of the steamer's passengers and crew.

A remotely-operated vehicle photographed dishware sitting in what was once the Portland's *kitchen. Photo credit: NOAA Stellwagen Bank National Marine Sanctuary, Northeast Underwater Research, Technology and Education Center and the Science Channel.*

The multi-masted coal schooners *Frank A. Palmer* and *Louise B. Crary* collided on December 17 1902 and their connected remains lie in the deep waters of the Sanctuary. The two Maine-built vessels represent some of the largest 19th century coastal trading vessels. Each vessel is still loaded with 3000 tons (2722 metric tons) of coal shipped from Virginia. Within minutes of the collision, six of the 21 sailors lost their lives when the schooners plummeted to the bottom. The remaining 15 sailors made it into *Frank A. Palmer's* lifeboat. During the following four nights, five more men perished from exposure in the open boat before being rescued 60 miles (97 kilometers) off Cape Cod, Massachusetts. The schooners now sit upright on the Sanctuary's seafloor. The vessels are in an excellent state of preservation, providing researchers a unique opportunity to explore two similar vessels at one location.

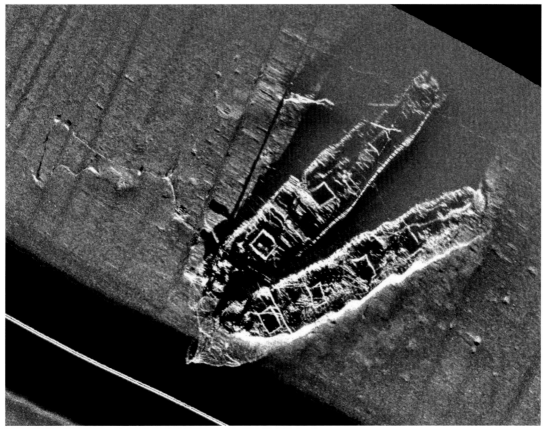

A side scan sonar image shows the collided schooners Frank A. Palmer *and* Louise B. Crary *still locked together at their bows. Photo credit: NOAA Stellwagen Bank National Marine Sanctuary and Northeast Underwater Research, Technology and Education Center.*

Paul Palmer, another coal schooner that ended up as a sanctuary shipwreck, was a very unlucky ship. The 276-foot (84-meter) long, five-masted vessel departed Rockport, Maine on Friday the 13th in June 1913 without a cargo. Two days later it was on fire off Race Point, Massachusetts. The crew was unable to quench the blaze, and although the captain, crew and passengers escaped unharmed, the ship burned to its water line and sank. Today the *Paul Palmer*'s remains lie partially buried on a flat sandy stretch on the top of Stellwagen Bank.

The remains of the eastern rig dragger *Joffre* lie in over 300 feet (91 meters) of water off Gloucester, Massachusetts. *Joffre*'s extant remains consist of its lower hull structure, propulsion components, vessel hardware, and fishing gear. The *Joffre* was built as an auxiliary schooner in Essex, Massachusetts in 1918. Initially, *Joffre* entered the mackerel seine fishery, but within a year, its owners set the schooner after groundfish. During the 1920s, *Joffre*'s crew landed record catches of halibut. After dory trawling for haddock and halibut for nearly twenty years, *Joffre*'s new captain, Simon Theriault, converted the 105-foot (32-meter) long vessel into an eastern rig dragger to pursue Acadian Redfish, a rapidly developing fishery. *Joffre*'s working life spans the mechanization of New England's fisheries and exemplifies the transition from sail to diesel power. During its 29-year career it landed more than 15 million pounds (6.8 million kilograms) of fish. On the evening of August 9, 1947, as it was returning to Gloucester, Massachusetts after a routine ten-day fishing trip to Nova Scotia's offshore banks, the *Joffre*'s engine caught fire. The flames quickly engulfed the wheelhouse and engine spaces forcing the ten-man crew to abandon ship into dories without gathering their personal effects. Despite efforts to quench the blaze and tow the vessel to port, the *Joffre* sank the next morning.

An anchor sits at the Joffre's *bow among scattered debris. Photo credit: NOAA/Stellwagen Bank National Marine Sanctuary and Northeast Underwater Research, Technology and Education Center.*

The *Edna G.* was a 54-foot (16.5-meter) groundfishing vessel launched in 1956 by the Morehead City Shipbuilding Corporation of Morehead City, North Carolina. The vessel sank on June 30, 1988, off Gloucester, Massachusetts, as her two-man crew set out its trawl net. A strange noise alerted the crew to water rapidly filling *Edna G.*'s engine room. The fishermen were able to abandon ship and were picked up by another fishing vessel. The exact cause of the sinking was never determined. The shipwreck was documented in 2003, with the use of a remotely-operated vehicle. The shipwreck represents a rapidly disappearing watercraft variety emblematic of the region's maritime traditions.

Edna G.'s wooden hull was almost completely intact aside from a hole on its portside under the pilothouse. This hole likely caused the vessel to sink. Photo credit: NOAA Stellwagen Bank National Marine Sanctuary, Northeast Underwater Research, Technology and Education Center, and the Science Channel.

Key species within the Sanctuary

MARINE MAMMALS

Stellwagen Bank serves as a sumptuous smorgasbord for marine mammals. Of particular importance is the wealth of sand lance (also known as sand eels) that burrow into the coarse sands of the bank. Schools of these fatty (calorie-rich) fish provide excellent nutrition for the whales (as well as larger fish and sea birds) that feed in these waters all summer.

A school of sand lance swims in the open waters of the sanctuary. Photo credit: Matthew Lawrence, NOAA/ Stellwagen Bank National Marine Sanctuary.

Some 22 species of marine mammals have been seen in Stellwagen Bank National Marine Sanctuary at one time or another, but there are several species that are regular visitors. These species are: humpback whale, fin whale, minke whale, North Atlantic right whale, Atlantic white-sided dolphin, common dolphin, harbor porpoise, pilot whale, and harbor seal.

Breeching Humpback Whale
Stellwagen Bank National Marine Sanctuary

Henry Lynch
stellwagen.noaa.gov

One humpback whale breaches as another rounds out into a dive in Stellwagen Bank National Marine Sanctuary. Photo credit: Henry Lynch.

LOBSTERS

The magnificent Maine lobster is, we'd been warned, the new clawed kingpin in a lop-sided ecosystem absent of giant cod. Up until 50 years ago, big finfish were the keystone predators of the northwestern Atlantic coastal ecosystem, consuming and controlling populations of lobsters and other seafloor invertebrates residing on a lower link in the food web. But the collapse of the ground fisheries—haddock, pollock, wolffish and the Atlantic cod—released armored crustaceans from 4,000 years of top-down predation. Now they are rising up to fill the empty niches. Still, the brazen behavior of these lobsters roaming across an open landscape devoid of shelter surprises us and adds yet another eerie element to this unfamiliar benthos.

The American lobster of Stellwagen Bank National Marine Sanctuary. Photo credit: Carrie Vonderhaar, Ocean Futures Society.

Pulling lobster traps on board The Resolve. *Photo credit: Carrie Vonderhaar, Ocean Futures Society.*

An American lobster defiantly displays its claws. Photo credit: Carrie Vonderhaar, Ocean Futures Society.

"Lobster is the biggest single fishing industry in the Northeast," according to the Massachusetts Lobsterman's Association and in 1996, accounted for 25 percent of all fishing revenue and was valued at $242 million and supported about 50,000 jobs. The commercial lobster fishing industry in Massachusetts has been carefully managed for decades, and the catch per unit effort has reached an all time high in the Gulf of Maine.

In 1992, 57 million pounds (26 million kilograms) of lobsters were landed in the U.S. and approximately 90 percent came from Massachusetts, Rhode Island and Maine.

As the executive director of The Lobster Conservancy, Diane Cowan tracks the life cycles of lobsters that migrate widely around the Gulf of Maine, some for over 110 miles (177 kilometers) from Friendship to the tip of Cape Cod. American lobsters, she explains, are capable of reflex amputation—the ability to drop a claw or other body part as an escape defense mechanism. These limbs eventually grow back but during the interim, the loss of a large claw can hinder the lobster's survival.

Each of the crustacean's two claws is evolutionarily engineered for slightly different purposes. The larger one is called a "crusher claw" and it has slow twitch muscles, which are used to crack open shellfish prey, like clams and mussels and sea urchins. The second claw, called a "pincher" is shaped more like a pair of scissors and its fast twitch muscles can seize fish right out of the water.

"And lobsters are very olfactory," Diane explains. "They have a highly developed sense of smell that is similar in comparison with canines. In fact, more than sight, lobsters rely upon chemosensory organs on the first antennae on the front of their heads that function as a 'nose' and the tiny hairs covering their antennules, to find a meal." The lobster's keen sense of smell also serves an additional function—it can help with finding a mate. Both male and female lobsters secrete sex pheromones, Diane explains to Jean-Michel, "which act as sex attractants or as signals necessary for pair formation."

Lobsters have five pairs of legs, each adapted to serve unique functions, from walking, finding food and grooming to housing the reproductive organs. Their fan-like, six-segmented tail is adorned with delicate swimmerets, which aid in copulation and are also where the eggs are attached. An adult one-pound (450-gram) female lobster, Diane explains, can carry 8,000 eggs. But females as big and old as one 35-year-old specimen are super-breeders that can carry more than 100,000 eggs, which the mother must brood for nine to 13 months before hatching. Large females also produce larger offspring.

Diane Cowan points out a female lobster's egg clutch. Photo credit: Carrie Vonderhaar, Ocean Futures Society.

Emerging Environmental Issues

A sanctuary diver cuts part of a derelict net draped over the Paul Palmer's *windlass. Photo credit: NOAA/ Stellwagen Bank National Marine Sanctuary.*

Perhaps no other sanctuary better exemplifies the consequences of human impact than Stellwagen Bank. It is a cautionary tale of exploitation and fishing down the food chain. But the effects are reaching beyond a single species. For example, the team saw how the sea is criss-crossed with lobster pots and gillnets and how these could impact the whales that share these waters. They also experienced the unique richness of this part of the sea and the plans to save it.

BOAT TRAFFIC AND WHALES

Today, Sanctuary researchers are studying the amount and type of vessel traffic that passes through the region, and how that traffic might be better informed to protect marine mammals in Sanctuary waters. Cargo ships, oil tankers, cruise liners and other large vessels funnel through the shipping lanes in and out of Boston Harbor thousands of times every year. The route takes them through waters where high concentrations of humpback, North Atlantic right, and other whales are found, putting both the whales and ships at risk of dangerous collisions.

Numerous large ships travel through the Sanctuary where whales feed. Photo credit: Whale Center of New England & Stellwagen Bank National Marine Sanctuary (photo taken under NOAA Fisheries Permit # 981-1707-00).

To reduce the potential for such accidents, the United Nations International Maritime Organization shifted the shipping lanes in 2007 based on research initiated by the Sanctuary and with data supplied by several whale research groups in the area. The accepted recommendation, put forth by the Sanctuary, NOAA Fisheries and the U.S. Coast Guard, redirected vessel traffic 12 degrees to the north to an area with fewer whales. The resulting plan increased travel time for ships by just 10-22 minutes, but cut down the risk of collisions with critically endangered North Atlantic right whales by an estimated 58 percent and all other baleen whales by 81 percent.

To further protect North Atlantic right whales, the Right Whale Listening Network employs 13 "auto-detection buoys" that listen for calling whales day and night. The buoys have an estimated listening radius of five nautical miles (5.8 miles). A line of 10 buoys provides full coverage for a 55-mile (88-kilometer) stretch of the commercial shipping lanes into and out of Boston Harbor (four of these buoys are within Stellwagen Bank National Marine Sanctuary); three additional buoys are in Cape Cod Bay. The buoys record underwater sounds and analyze them as the sounds come in. When the onboard software determines that a call may be from a North Atlantic right whale, the system makes a satellite call to an analyst at the Bioacoustics Research Center at Cornell University, who verifies the identification. The information is then sent to ships in the area, posted online[2] and made available through an iPad and iPhone software application.

Researchers Fred Wenzel of NOAA Fisheries (l) and David Wiley of the Stellwagen Bank National Marine Sanctuary (r) prepare to moor a passive acoustic buoy to the ocean bottom on Stellwagen Bank. The project is a joint effort among researchers from NOAA Fisheries Woods Hole, MA; Stellwagen Bank National Marine Sanctuary; and Cornell University's Laboratory of Ornithology. Photo credit: Michael Thompson, Stellwagen Bank National Marine Sanctuary.

ENTANGLEMENT OF WHALES IN FISHING GEAR

The eastern seaboard of the United States is the most heavily utilized ocean habitat in the world. Pollution and ship strikes are taking their toll on whales and an increasing number of fishing gear entanglements are having equally deadly consequences, as fishers and whales target the same productive zones of the ocean. While it's not always clear what types of fishing gear may be causing entanglements, as many as 10 different mobile and fixed gear fisheries operate at Stellwagen.

Scarring on whales indicates that 10 to 25 percent of humpbacks venturing into the Gulf of Maine become entangled each year. The Provincetown Center for Coastal

---

2   http://www.listenforwhales.org

Studies found that female whales exhibiting evidence of fishing gear scars produced far fewer calves than did those without scars. The American Cetacean Society has reported more than 60 percent of North Atlantic right whales have entanglement scars and at least two North Atlantic right whale deaths in the past three years can be directly linked to fishing gear.

The tail of this North Atlantic right whale shows scars from past entanglement in fishing gear. Photo credit: Beth Josephson, NOAA/Northeast Fisheries Science Center.

The trail of evidence found on entangled whales is what researchers rely upon to understand what is occurring far from view. Baleen whales foraging near the seafloor are catching lower jaws and flippers in the nearly invisible floating loops. Once trapped, the panicked whales will attempt to spin and twist themselves free, but only become more deeply ensnared, like flies caught in a spider web. Some whales drown, but those that are able to surface and swim may end up towing hundreds of pounds of fishing gear and traps for months or years. As a result, entangled whales may not be able to breed, which means they can no longer be counted as part of the reproductive population. Others suffer deformities from the tourniquet of constricting lines and eventually die from injuries or starvation.

A handful of fortunate animals are freed each year through the efforts of trained, permitted rescuers who attempt to track entangled whales in a vast ocean. When (and if) an injured whale is located, the 30- to 50-ton (27- to 45-metric ton) animal must first be slowed and prevented from diving before any aid can be rendered. Rescuers will attach buoys and sea anchors to keep the whale at the surface, then attempt to cut away the tangle of gear.

A crew works to disentangle a North Atlantic right whale off the coast of Georgia in 2009. Photo credit: Georgia Department of Natural Resources and Florida Fish and Wildlife Conservation Commission under NOAA Permit No. 9321489 under the authority of the U.S. Endangered Species Act and Marine Mammal Protection Act.

Growing public awareness over the harm fishing gear entanglements cause whales, sea turtles, dolphins and basking sharks led to a 2004 initiative to try and lessen the risks. The International Fund for Animal Welfare and the Massachusetts Lobstermen's Association teamed up in a unique collaborative partnership to secure funding through Congress to launch a voluntary buy-back initiative that would eliminate deadly floating lines in Massachusetts Bay. Nearly 70 percent of the $10,000 cost per fishing vessel was covered in the buyback, which allowed fishermen to replace old floating lines with either neutrally buoyant or traditional sinking lines for their traps.

Part science, part hope, gear modifications like these, it's widely believed, will be a major step towards reducing whale entanglements without a heavy penalty to fishermen.

OVERFISHING

IN 1526, early Portuguese explorers who endured the trans-Atlantic crossing were so in awe of the abundance of enormous fish they encountered that they labeled their charts with the reference "the land of cod," according to Robert Steneck, a University of Maine research scientist. Searching historical archives and archaeological middens, Steneck, along with other fisheries biologists, are attempting to step back in time to try and find a historic baseline for cod populations in New England's waters. What they are uncovering seems almost as mythical in scale as the etchings of giant fish with bulbous eyes and enormous mouths that danced among the waves adorning the early European charts.

Atlantic cod swim around a sanctuary shipwreck. Credit: Doug Costa, Stellwagen Bank National Marine Sanctuary.

Archaeological evidence along Maine's shoreline dating as far back as 4,500 years ago indicates the diets of coastal Native Americans consisted mostly of seafood. Europeans arriving to the shores of North America were quick to exploit a fresh reserve of fish. By the year 1508, 10 percent of the salt cod found in Portuguese markets was being imported from the New World. Within forty-two years, nearly 60 percent of all of the fish eaten in Europe was New England or Newfoundland cod.

New England's commercial cod fishing industry "gold rush" had reached an epic scale by the turn of the century. According to Steneck, it was further fueled by "mechanized fishing technology and onboard refrigeration [which] enabled the targeting of spawning aggregations." This final assault on stocks is what scientists believe, "led to the rapid decline in the numbers and body size of coastal cod in the Gulf of Maine."

By the 1940s, the extirpation of cod along with other giant finfishes like pollock, haddock and salmon meant apex predators had been functionally removed from the ecosystem and, as a result, coastal food webs were widely altered. By analyzing the logs of fishing fleets that had worked the Scotian Shelf during 1852, researchers have been able to determine that the biomass of cod remaining today is only three to four percent of what it was 150 years ago. And this percentage, researchers point out, is derived from a population baseline heavily impacted by fishing that had been occurring since the early 1500s.

Now all but a lingering memory, the schools of giant fish are gone. New England's fishing fleets teeter on the verge of economic collapse as boats lie idle amidst the closure of 400-year-old fishing grounds with few, if any, solutions to restore the groundfish stocks that have all gone the way of the buffalo.

George's Bank crew hand-line fishing, gaffing fish over the rail and cutting out tongues. Drawing by H. W. Elliott and Capt. J. W. Collins. Image credit: NOAA Fisheries.

Baskets of cod and haddock await processing. Photo credit: NOAA.

Research within the Sanctuary

- **Getting a Whale's-Eye View in Stellwagen Bank**: A team of government and university scientists is peering into the depths of Stellwagen Bank National Marine Sanctuary in an attempt to better understand whale behavior and the underwater world they inhabit. The primary tool they are using is the Dtag—a small data collection package that attaches to the whale with suction cups. This non-invasive tag records direction, pitch, roll, sounds heard and made by the animal. Once the Dtag pops off (either programmed or naturally) the equipment is retrieved and the data downloaded. After processing the numbers, the researchers are able to produce images that show the tracks of the whales, making the ocean transparent for these behavior studies. In addition to the static pictures, the data can be manipulated to make visualizations—a form of moving image. A few realistic animations have even been created. The Sanctuary has also teamed with National Geographic and its Crittercam[3]—a video camera that also uses a similar suction cup attachment to a subject whale. Video footage has revealed new aspects of whale feeding and has given clues about how the whales are catching their prey. Additional studies use a towed sonar system to study prey fields (the extent and density of fish, primarily sand lance). An extra project involves the collection of humpback whale dung (also referred to as "poop"). From these leavings, scientists can learn about the diet and health of the whale. The primary use of the dung samples is to continue studies on nitrogen cycling in the ocean.

---

3   http://animals.nationalgeographic.com/animals/crittercam/

A whale researcher from the Stellwagen Bank research team carefully places a suction cup mounted acoustic recording tag on a humpback whale to study its underwater behaviors. Photo credit: NOAA/Stellwagen Bank National Marine Sanctuary.

- **Movement of Atlantic Cod:** Atlantic cod populations in the Gulf of Maine have been exploited commercially for several hundred years, and continue to be heavily fished today. Scientists have collaborated on a research project using acoustic telemetry technology to quantify cod movement over different features of the landscape. The high site fidelity of many cod to individual piled boulder reefs suggests that habitat-specific management measures, such as marine reserves, may offer significant protection to cod within the Sanctuary. The successful conservation and management of cod in the Gulf of Maine, and at the scale of Stellwagen Bank National Marine Sanctuary in particular, is highly dependent on this information.

Another project is recording the vocalizations of cod and other demersal fish to determine possible spawning grounds and movement within the study area.

- **Archeological Research:** Stellwagen Bank National Marine Sanctuary researchers use a variety of tools and techniques to locate and document shipwreck sites. Since the Sanctuary's seafloor lies at depths ranging from 65 to 600 feet (20 to 183 meters), sophisticated equipment is often needed to conduct archaeological research. Sanctuary maritime archaeologists have used SCUBA, side scan sonar, remotely-operated vehicles (ROVs), and autonomous underwater vehicles (AUVs). The Sanctuary's archaeological research seeks to explore the Sanctuary's heritage resources residing on its seafloor and interpret the physical reminders of past events to allow the public a greater understanding of its maritime legacy.

Side scan sonar is used by scientists to map the Sanctuary's seafloor. Photo credit: Stellwagen Bank National Marine Sanctuary.

- **International Partnerships:** NOAA and the government of the Dominican Republic created the first international agreement to protect an endangered whale at both ends of its migratory route when a sister sanctuary program was initiated. Stellwagen Bank National Marine Sanctuary, the humpbacks' northern feeding ground, and the Marine Mammal Sanctuary of the Dominican Republic, their southern calving and breeding ground, both shelter a shared resource. Exchanges of research expertise and educational programs have furthered conservation at both sites. In 2011, the government of France signed a similar agreement with the Stellwagen Bank Sanctuary, enlarging the areas covered under the sister sanctuary program into the French Antilles. The British Overseas Territory of Bermuda has also pledged to protect these endangered North Atlantic humpback whales through a Letter of Intent, signed in 2011. Bermuda sits along the migratory corridor, creating a "benevolent Bermuda Triangle" between the humpbacks' winter breeding and calving grounds to the south and their summer feeding grounds to the north. Stellwagen Bank and the sister sanctuaries will exchange photos of whale flukes for humpback population studies and related research; share information, data, and experiences in managing marine mammal protected areas; and coordinate research, education, and strategies for engaging their local communities in whale conservation.

Research Assets

R/V *AUK*

The 50-foot (15-meter) Research Vessel *Auk* is used for a variety of research projects, as well as for emergency response, enforcement, and education/outreach missions. The catamaran, with its two-hulls, provides a stable platform that maximizes deck space while providing room for wet and dry laboratories and berthing areas for overnight cruises. A flying bridge offers better opportunities for marine mammal observations, and winches, an A-frame and dive ladders will accommodate various mission tasks.

The NOAA Research Vessel Auk *departs Scituate Harbor for a cruise dedicated to scientific study of the sanctuary. Photo credit: Anne Smrcina, NOAA/Stellwagen Bank National Marine Sanctuary.*

ROVS AND AUVS

Shipwrecks in deep sections of the Sanctuary are explored with remotely-operated vehicles (ROVs). ROVs are tethered robots that "fly" through the water, allowing Sanctuary scientists to spend hours gathering archaeological data without being limited by the cold water, air supply, and depths. Equipped with lights and video cameras, ROVs are launched and controlled from a research vessel positioned above the shipwreck. Archaeologists study the video transmitted through the tether to determine the age, characteristics, and possible identity of the shipwreck.

For investigations in deeper waters where diving is not possible, sanctuary researchers use equipment, such as this remotely-operated vehicle (ROV). Photo credit: Anne Smrcina, NOAA/Stellwagen Bank National Marine Sanctuary.

The newest technology used by the Sanctuary is an autonomous underwater vehicle (AUV). AUV's are un-tethered robots programmed to maneuver along a predetermined path and fulfill a specific function, such as taking photographs or sampling the water. After the AUV completes its mission, it returns to the surface where researchers retrieve the vehicle and download the data collected during the mission. AUVs used by the Sanctuary to investigate maritime heritage resources have been outfitted with downward facing cameras to gather images that can be pieced together to build a photomosaic.

Visiting the Sanctuary

Note: In the last section of the book, "When You Visit the Sanctuaries," is detailed information about resources found within each sanctuary to help visitors have an enjoyable and productive visit.

Gerry E. Studds Stellwagen Bank National Marine Sanctuary provides numerous ocean-based activities that can entertain everyone from the wildlife-watching novice to the expert diver. Visitors to the Sanctuary can take excursion boats from numerous local areas to watch marine wildlife, particularly whales. The site has been named one of the ten top whale-watching sites in the world in several listings. Other tourist possibilities include fishing excursions or, for experienced divers, dive trips to the bank by commercial operations. Several nearby aquariums and museums in the Sanctuary region feature Stellwagen Bank displays. In 2012 the Sanctuary and its friends group, Stellwagen Alive, initiated a cell phone audio message tour with stops at numerous points along the coast. Stellwagen Bank provides everything from glimpses of endangered whales to learning opportunities at numerous museums and aquariums.

The New England Aquarium has exhibits featuring the Sanctuary. Photo credit: Stellwagen Bank National Marine Sanctuary.

VISITOR'S CENTER

While Stellwagen Bank National Marine Sanctuary does not have its own visitor's center, it has exhibits at several area attractions. Of particular note are the tanks in the cold water gallery at the New England Aquarium and the Stellwagen Sanctuary Hall in Maritime Gloucester, a museum located along the historic waterfront of America's first fishing port. Other exhibits include a kiosk at Mac-Millan Wharf (Provincetown, Massachusetts), a shipwreck exhibit at the Scituate Maritime and Irish Mossing Museum (Scituate, Massachusetts), whale conservation exhibits at the Cape Cod National Seashore Province Lands Visitor Center (Provincetown, Massachusetts) and Halibut Point State Park Vistor Center (Rockport, Massachusetts), displays at the Cape Cod Museum of Natural History (Cape Cod, Massachusetts), and exhibit panels and aquarium displays at the Woods Hole Science Aquarium (Woods Hole, Massachusetts).

An informational kiosk on sanctuary resources has been placed at MacMillan Wharf in Provincetown, a center for whale watching on Cape Cod. Photo credit: Brad Barr/Stellwagen Bank National Marine Sanctuary.

SANCTUARY OFFICE LOCATION

Stellwagen Bank National Marine Sanctuary's headquarters offices are located in Scituate, Massachusetts. The facility consists of the main building, a meeting annex, and a boathouse with dock. The facility was the third NOAA building in the nation to incorporate a geo-thermal heating and cooling system. This HVAC system reduces the dependency on fossil fuels by using the earth as a heat source in the winter and a heat sink in the summer.

175 Edward Foster Road
Scituate, Massachusetts 02066
Telephone: 781-545-8026

BOATING

The Sanctuary is open to all forms of vessels, from sailboats to large, ocean-going freighters, tankers and cruise liners. Boaters should remain vigilant to avoid interfering with fishing gear, or colliding with other boaters or marine animals such as whales, sea turtles, and basking sharks. In particular, boaters should familiarize themselves with the regional whale watching guidelines[4] to avoid harmful encounters with marine mammals. The Sanctuary recommends that boaters limit their vessel's speed to 14 knots to allow for sufficient time to avoid a marine animal that suddenly appears.

---

4   http://stellwagen.noaa.gov/visit/whalewatching/guidelines.html

Whale watching in Stellwagen Bank National Marine Sanctuary. Photo credit: Anne Smrcina, NOAA/ Stellwagen Bank National Marine Sanctuary.

Stellwagen Bank National Marine Sanctuary is a busy place with an active commercial fishing fleet, many seasonal whale watch vessels, and hundreds of cargo ships heading to or leaving from Boston Harbor. Weather and sea conditions[5] can change quickly, turning a clear day with calm waters into a dense pea soup or a rollercoaster ride. The prudent mariner cruises or sails into the Sanctuary only after taking all possible precautions, including checking weather forecasts, equipping the boat with an emergency signaling device and two-way radio, leaving a float plan with a responsible individual on shore, and making

5   http://stellwagen.noaa.gov/visit/weatherandsea.html

sure that all individuals on board have life preservers (and wear them whenever possible). Even better, survival suits and life rafts should also be thought of as essential equipment (especially when venturing out in months other than mid-summer).

Petty Officer Kevinn Smith demonstrates to a class of students and their parents the importance of wearing the proper sized life jacket. Photo credit: Petty Officer Gail Sinner, U.S. Coast Guard.

Boating access points[6] and locations of boat pumpout stations[7] can be found online.

---

6   http://stellwagen.noaa.gov/visit/boating/accesspoints.html
7   http://stellwagen.noaa.gov/visit/boating/pumpout.html

See A Spout, Watch Out! is a boater education program designed to make recreational boaters aware of ways to keep themselves and whales safer. By following these six simple, catchy tips, boaters will not be in danger of violating the Marine Mammal Protection Act and the Endangered Species Act. The program is offered by the Sanctuary, NOAA Fisheries and the Whale and Dolphin Conservation Society. The six tips are:

1-See A Spout, Watch Out!

If you see a spout, or a tail, or a breaching whale, please slow down and post a lookout. Some whales dive 20 minutes or more searching for food. If you've seen one whale, many more could be close-maybe too close to your boat and its spinning propellers. Proceed cautiously!

2-Head On Is Wrong!

Don't alter a whale's path by cutting it off or risk striking a whale by approaching too closely. Please comply with regional regulations and guidelines when watching whales. This information is found on the websites of the sponsoring organizations. Be aware that federal regulations and Massachusetts laws prohibit approaching the highly endangered North Atlantic right whale closer than 500 yards (457 meters).

3-Lots Of Boats, Then Talk To Folks!

If there are other boats watching or traveling near whales, hail them on your VHF radio (channels 9 or 16) and coordinate your viewing efforts.

4-Avoid Troubles, Steer Clear of Bubbles!

Humpback whales create "bubble clouds" and "bubble nets" to corral schools of small fish. Never approach or drive through a bubble cloud or net. A feeding whale is likely to be just below the surface.

5-Don't Chase, Give The Whales Space!

Closely approaching a whale may cause the animal to move away from its food source. Respect the whale and keep your distance. If a whale moves away, don't chase it. A cautious boater may get to see whales feeding, breaching or tail and flipper slapping. Enjoy the whales; don't endanger them or yourselves.

6—Drop Your Sails When Watching Whales!

A boat under sail may not be able to reduce speed or stop at a safe distance from a surfacing whale. When in the vicinity of whales, it is best to use your auxiliary motor and proceed cautiously.

FISHING

For over 400 years, Massachusetts Bay has been a destination for fishing activities. The area was first fished by Native Americans who collected a variety of marine foods along the water's edge. During the colonial period, fish played a large role as one of the region's main export commodities. The Pilgrims came to Plymouth Colony with the intention of fishing, and many 17th century towns grew and prospered from this industry. As technology progressed, fishing vessels and fishing methods evolved to meet the demands of the market. The small rowed craft of the colonial period were replaced by swift schooners in the 18th and 19th century which were then replaced by engine driven trawlers in the 20th century. Today, fishermen travel from their home ports for Stellwagen Bank to harvest finfish and shellfish.

Dann Blackwood, USGS

Recreational and commercial fishing boats have easy access to the sanctuary from Cape Cod and Cape Ann. Boston, pictured here, is just 25 miles directly west. Photo credit: Dann Blackwood, USGS.

Recreational fishing is a popular activity in the Sanctuary, with individuals visiting the Sanctuary via private vessels and charter/party boats. Fishermen and women target a variety of species that use the different types of habitats found there.[8] A saltwater angler permit is needed for recreational fishing in the Sanctuary and all federal waters, although most state saltwater permits qualify as a substitute for the federal version. In addition, several federal regulations have been established that address fishing activities in the Sanctuary.[9] Anglers should be aware that fishing for striped bass and several species of sharks is illegal in federal waters.

There are many charter fishing companies operating in ports and harbors along the coast. Recreational fishing parties should use care in planning trips into the Sanctuary, as weather and sea conditions can change quickly and drastically. Boaters should check marine forecasts before departure.

Circle hooks can reduce catch-and-release mortality.
Photo credit: NOAA Fisheries.

8   http://stellwagen.noaa.gov/visit/fishingrec/species.html
9   http://stellwagen.noaa.gov/visit/fishingrec/regulations.html

The Massachusetts Division of Marine Fisheries is actively encouraging the use of circle hooks. The use of circle hooks is promoted in fisheries that use baited hooks for the capture of striped bass, tunas, and other species where these hooks can effectively reduce the mortality of released fish. Two recent research projects focused on the use of circle hooks when using bait for striped bass and tunas. In those experiments circle hooks showed a reduction in the rate of potential lethal wounding, and subsequent mortality when compared to J-hooks. Researchers have also estimated the effectiveness of circle hooks to hook fish that took natural baits. Results indicate that circle hooks catch slightly more fish than J-hooks.

DIVING

The Sanctuary offers experienced SCUBA divers a chance to explore an offshore environment at that has only recently gained the attention of the dive community. Exposed waters create challenging dive conditions, but offer rewarding experiences. Surprisingly, fifteen percent of the Sanctuary, or 126 square miles (326 square kilometers), is shallower than 130 feet (40 meters) at low tide. Much of this area lies atop Stellwagen Bank, but also includes southern Jeffreys Ledge and the top of Sanctuary Hill. Diving offshore is unlike diving at a similar depth inshore. In addition to the deep water, divers will likely experience strong currents at the surface and the bottom, especially if the wind and tide are moving in the same direction. Divers should plan their dives around slack tide for the best underwater and surface conditions.

Anemones and other invertebrates cover a wreck being investigated by a diver. Photo credit: Matthew Lawrence, NOAA/Stellwagen Bank National Marine Sanctuary.

The tide station at Boston Light or Race Point will provide an estimation of slack tide at Stellwagen Bank. Slack tide on Stellwagen Bank usually occurs 30 minutes before the calculated high or low tides reported for those tide stations. Slack tide for Jeffreys Ledge and Sanctuary Hill is best indicated by the tide station at Rockport. It is essential that dive boats fly both a red and white diver down flag and the blue and white international dive flag since the Sanctuary is frequently transited by both American and foreign-flagged ships. Also divers should be aware that the shipping lanes for vessels coming into and out of the port of Boston pass through the Sanctuary.

An ocean sunfish swims directly over a Sanctuary shipwreck while divers explore in the distance.
Photo credit: Matthew Lawrence, NOAA/Stellwagen Bank National Marine Sanctuary.

Under Sanctuary regulations, it is illegal to move, remove, or injure or attempt to move, remove, or injure a Sanctuary historical resource. Divers are not permitted to grapple a shipwreck, drop a down line directly onto a shipwreck, or tie a down line onto any part of a shipwreck. Divers are also not allowed to leave an unattended mooring in the Sanctuary at any time. Diving when in the vicinity of whales is considered harassment, and is punishable under federal law. Any boating activity that harms or causes a whale to change its behavior is also a violation of the Marine Mammal Protection Act and the Endangered Species Act.

In addition to standard scuba gear, divers should consider carrying a reel and lift bag to make ascents if separated from their down line and a safety sausage and whistle or other surface signaling devices. A completely redundant air supply is also advisable. Since the seafloor water temperature rarely rises above 50°F (10°C), drysuits make diving safer and more comfortable. A hazard divers may encounter is fishing gear. Gill nets in the water column pose the greatest threat to divers because they are hard to see and are difficult to remove if a diver gets entangled in one. Additionally, derelict fishing gear such as monofilament line, masses of lobster pots and lines, and lost trawl nets can also ensnare divers. Divers need to be particularly aware of their surroundings if close to boats actively fishing since those boats might not be aware of divers under the water. It is wise for divers to carry a second knife or cutting device so they can free themselves if they become entangled and cannot reach their primary cutting tool.

A derelict fishing net wraps around the Paul Palmer's *large steam windlass.*
Photo credit: Matthew Lawrence, NOAA/Stellwagen Bank National Marine Sanctuary.

Divers venturing into frigid waters learn to appreciate two common physiological responses to the cold: instant pain, a sensation Blair[10] euphemistically describes "as the ice pick to the forehead experience;" and a rapid gasp for breath, the result of air being forced from the diaphragm and a feeling of gripping asphyxia. Given enough thermal protection, both of these reflexes last only a few fleeting seconds before the mind establishes reason over the body's coldwater shock response associated with imminent death.

WHALE WATCHING

One of the important ecotourism industries in eastern Massachusetts is whale watching, with an estimated one million passengers heading out onto the ocean to view some of the largest animals on our planet. Most of those sea-going trips head out to Stellwagen Bank National Marine Sanctuary. A number of companies schedule regular trips into the Sanctuary. Stellwagen Bank is one of the best places to observe feeding humpback whales in the United States.

Humpback whales feeding. Photo credit: Stellwagen Bank National Marine Sanctuary.

To report a stranded, injured, entangled or dead marine mammal or sea turtle, call 866-755-NOAA (2266) or contact the U.S. Coast Guard via VHF channel 16. If possible, please stay by an entangled whale until a response vessel arrives. If you must depart, document your sighting with photos or video and report the time, location and whale's direction of travel when you left the scene. To report presumed marine law violations, call NOAA's Office of Law Enforcement at 800-853-1964.

---

10   Blair Mott, chief diver, Ocean Futures Society

BIRD WATCHING

While Stellwagen Bank National Marine Sanctuary has gained fame as a world-class whale watching destination, it can also claim the distinction of being an exciting location for bird watching. The same qualities that make the Sanctuary an ideal site for spotting whales make it an excellent bird-watching area as well. More than 40 species of seabirds regularly come to these waters to feed on the abundant fish, plankton, and other marine invertebrates.[11,12] Massachusetts Audubon successfully nominated Stellwagen Bank as an Important Bird Area. This program, organized by BirdLife International, is part of a global effort to identify and conserve areas that are vital to birds and other biodiversity.

Greater shearwater. Photo credit: Stellwagen Bank National Marine Sanctuary.

---

11   http://stellwagen.noaa.gov/visit/birdwatching/seasonalstatus.html
12   http://stellwagen.noaa.gov/visit/birdwatching/species.html

Monitor

About Monitor *National Marine Sanctuary*

Designated in 1975, the one-square-mile (2.6-square-kilometer) *Monitor* National Marine Sanctuary was the nation's first marine sanctuary. It is also the only one dedicated to the preservation of a single cultural treasure, the wreck of the famed Civil War ironclad USS *Monitor*. The *Monitor* is recognized worldwide for its significance as a vessel that revolutionized 19th-century naval warfare technology and its famous battle at Hampton Roads with the Confederate warship CSS *Virginia* in 1862. Sinking in a storm off Cape Hatteras, North Carolina about nine months after this historic battle, and only eleven months after being launched, the *Monitor* remained lost beneath the waves for more than 100 years until its wreck was located in 1973.

The battle between the USS Monitor *and the Confederate Ironclad* Virginia *was the subject for a United States postage stamp in 1995. The* Monitor *is the vessel near the lower portion of the stamp. Image credit: United States Postal Service.*

The *Monitor* National Marine Sanctuary is located 16 miles (26 kilometers) south-south-east of the Cape Hatteras, North Carolina Lighthouse. Because of its location and environment it is impossible for the majority of the public to visit the *Monitor* National Marine Sanctuary.

The National Marine Sanctuary sites have not been designated for their ease of access but for their importance to the natural world or to human culture and history. The site of the USS Monitor *is one of the most inaccessible and required technology and dive expertise that was tested in difficult conditions and in deep water.*

Crew from the ship Grapple *in a rigid inflatable boat fight heavy seas in an attempt to connect the ship to one of the four mooring buoys. Photo credit:* Monitor 2001, Monitor *collection, NOAA/Ocean Exploration Program.*

Why a National Marine Sanctuary?

The *Monitor* has been called the most famous ship in American history. Its inventor, Swedish-American engineer John Ericsson, was anything but ordinary. The building of iron ships was not in itself revolutionary in the 1800s, but Ericsson was suggesting the use of iron as a protective plate rather than simply as a building material. In 1854 he presented a conceptual design of a steam-powered ironclad ship with rotating gun turret to Napoleon III of France. The concept, rejected by France, was accepted by the United States and would soon become the USS *Monitor*.

Photo of the Swedish engineer John Ericsson, taken around the time he was building the original Monitor. *Image Courtesy of The Mariners' Museum. Photo credit: The Mariner's Museum.*

Built in approximately 100 days at the Continental Ironworks in Greenpoint, New York, the *Monitor* was a technological feat. It was equipped with an Ericsson-designed screw propeller, steam engine and 21.5-foot (6.5-meter) diameter rotating gun turret. The turret was the first of its kind and turrets similar to Ericsson's design are still seen on modern warships. In a time when naval power traditionally consisted of wooden tall ships with gun ports, the *Monitor* was constructed of wood and plated with iron. The engineering spaces, crew and officer quarters and galley were all located below the water line, making it unique among ships built at that time.

Shortly after midnight on December 31, 1862, while under tow by the USS *Rhode Island* to Beaufort, North Carolina for repairs, the *Monitor* sank in a storm off Cape Hatteras, North Carolina. Sixteen crewmen lost their lives, most from being swept overboard while attempting to reach the lifeboats.

In 1973 a team of scientists aboard Duke University Research Vessel *Eastward* located the shipwreck remains of what they believed to be the USS *Monitor* lying upside down in 230 feet (70 meters) of water approximately 16 miles (26 kilometers) off Cape Hatteras, North Carolina. In 1974, they confirmed that the shipwreck was in fact the *Monitor*. During the expedition, scientists conducted extensive photography of the wreck from which the Naval Intelligence Division created the first photomosaic of the wreck.

Harper's Weekly *illustration of the launching of the USS* Monitor *on January 30, 1862 at Greenpoint, New York. Image credit:* Harpers' Weekly, *September 1862,* Monitor *Collection, NOAA.*

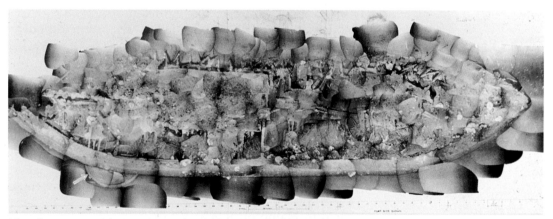

This photomosaic of the Monitor *was created in 1975. Image credit: NOAA.*

"When we found two sets of human remains in the turret, we realized immediately we were dealing with a war grave. The Navy requested that the remains be sent to the Central Identification Laboratory in Hawaii for forensic analysis. We hope someday to

A wedding ring was found on the left hand of Monitor *#2's remains. Photo credit:* Monitor *Collection, NOAA.*

identify the crewmen and we know there's the possibility that there may still be more seamen within the wreck."[1]

The shipwreck was designated the *Monitor* National Marine Sanctuary on January 30, 1975. The Sanctuary is comprised of a column of water extending from the ocean's surface to the seabed and is one nautical mile (1.15 mile/1.85 kilometers) in diameter.

Resources within the Monitor *National Marine Sanctuary*

USS *MONITOR*

Stealthy and nearly impregnable, the armor-plated USS Monitor *was the first of three ironclads commissioned by the United States Navy during the Civil War. Her futuristic design was the work of Swedish engineer John Ericsson and a radical departure from contemporary ships and sails of the day. Her 173-foot (53-meter)-long hull rode just below the waterline, thrust through the sea by one of the earliest marine propeller screws.*

The Ericsson Ironclad Battery Monitor *as illustrated in* Harper's Weekly, *March 22, 1862. Image credit:* Monitor *2001,* Monitor *Collection, NOAA/Ocean Exploration Program.*

In 1862, the USS Monitor *steamed into Hampton Roads, Virginia, to defend Union vessels that were under attack. Her newly designed rotating turret and Dahlgren cannons, many hoped, would serve the CSS* Virginia *her defeat.*

Ordered to Hampton Roads, Virginia, the USS *Monitor* arrived on the evening of March 8, 1862. The scene that greeted her crew that evening was horrifying. Previously that day, with the shore lined with cheering crowds of spectators and soldiers, CSS *Virginia* and her escorts had steamed down the

---

1   John Broadwater, *Monitor* National Marine Sanctuary manager

Elizabeth River. At anchor near Fort Monroe were the USS *Minnesota*, USS *Roanoke*, and USS *St. Lawrence* along with several gun-boats. Off the shores of Newport News, USS *Congress* and USS *Cumberland* were quietly moored, neither aware of the approaching *Virginia*.

As CSS *Virginia* made her maiden voyage into Hampton Roads that day, she proved the effectiveness of iron against wood. In less than an hour, the *Virginia* rammed and sank the *Cumberland*. The *Congress* was run aground and unable to effectively to bring her guns to bear on the *Virginia*. The *Congress* finally surrendered to end the slaughter. The fires started during the fight soon engulfed the ship in flames, which assured her complete destruction. The *Minnesota* was also badly damaged and aground. With two men killed and nineteen wounded, the *Virginia* steamed to Sewell's Point. Her smoke stack was pierced, her boat and anchors were shot away, and she had a leak from where her iron prow had broken away. Although she was a little worse for the wear, her armor had proved impregnable, verifying once and for all the great superiority of iron over wood.

As the *Monitor* anchored at 9:00 p.m., Lt. Worden, *Monitor's* Captain, was ordered to defend the *Minnesota*. The atmosphere on the *Monitor* was tense as the crew prepared for battle. No one got any sleep (not that they could have slept if they had wanted to) because the crew discovered that the turret mechanism had rusted from seawater. They spent the night lubricating and reworking the gears so that the turret would operate smoothly. This was not an easy process, as the 120-ton turret had to be jacked up so that the edge would clear the deck. The crew also had to remove the guns and their carriages along with the shot and powder. The *Monitor's* crew worked through the night, and as the sun rose over Hampton Roads, they were ready to meet their adversary.

Photograph of the crew on the deck of USS Monitor. *Image was taken on July 9, 1862 by James Gibson. Photo credit: Library of Congress.*

At about 7:30 a.m., on Sunday, March 9, 1862, the *Virginia* once again steamed out to re-engage the stranded *Minnesota*. Captain Worden knew what to do and steamed as far as possible away from the *Minnesota* before engaging in the first battle where iron would meet iron. For hours, the two armored warships fired upon each other, each side looking for their opponent's weaknesses. At times, the two vessels were touching, but the cannon shots bounced harmlessly off their iron armor. Almost four hours into the battle, a shot from the *Virginia* exploded against the forward side of the *Monitor*'s pilothouse, temporarily blinding Worden.

The *Monitor* pulled out of action to assess the damage to the ship. Lieutenant Catesby Jones, the *Virginia*'s commander, saw the *Monitor* leaving the battle. He assumed the *Virginia* had done serious damage to the Union ironclad and had forced her from the field. After two days of fighting, the Confederate ironclad had expended tons of coal and ammunition and the crew was exhausted. Jones gave the order for the *Virginia* to return to the navy yard to assess the damages.

Painting of the USS Monitor *and the CSS* Virginia's *battle in Hampton Roads on March 9, 1862. Image credit: Library of Congress.*

The *Monitor*, now under the command of Lt. Samuel D. Greene, left the shallow bay she had pulled in and steamed back into Hampton Roads. Seeing the *Virginia* heading towards the Elizabeth River and Norfolk, Greene assumed that the *Monitor* must have done serious damage to the *Virginia* and that she was retreating from the fight. As Greene's orders were to protect the *Minnesota*, he returned to her side until the wooden warship was floated on the next tide.

Although, the Battle of Hampton Roads was ultimately fought to a draw, the true significance of the engagement was that the era of the wooden warship was at an end. From that day forth, iron would forever rule the seas.

As the Monitor *continued to patrol the southeastern coast of the United States, her reputation for invincibility grew. Ericsson had designed her for river combat and shallow water coastal forays. Tragically, however her lack of seaworthiness in the open ocean was discovered far too late. On December 31, 1862, the battleship foundered during a heavy storm and was swamped by high waves while under tow by the* Rhode Island. *As she sank into the Atlantic Ocean off of Cape Hatteras, she was less than a year old.*

James River, Virginia. Officers on the Deck of the USS Monitor *near the turret. Taken July 9, 1862 (photo: James F. Gibson, b.1828). Image courtesy of United States Library of Congress.*

Approaching the *Monitor* on the first submersible dive in 1977, an archaeologist spotted a brass navigation lantern near the turret. This lantern has remained of particular interest because of its red Fresnel lens, evidence that it was a signal lantern. This is perhaps the same lantern Paymaster William Keeler mentions in his vivid account of watching the *Monitor's* red lantern as it vanished and reappeared on the dark, stormy ocean the night the ship sank.

The team listens as Jean-Michel Cousteau uses a model of the Monitor *to give filming directions. Photo credit: Carrie Vonderhaar, Ocean Futures Society.*

This red lantern was the first artifact recovered from the Monitor *National Marine Sanctuary. Photo credit: The Mariners' Museum.*

The Ocean Futures dive team (l-r: Matthew Ferraro, Chuck Davis and Blair Mott) with the anchor of the Monitor. *Artifacts like this anchor and the revolutionary turret (recovered in 2003) are part of the permanent collection of the Mariners' Museum in Newport News, Virginia. Photo credit: Carrie Vonderhaar, Ocean Futures Society.*

Major dives in 1979 recovered numerous small artifacts. The *Monitor's* unique four-fluked anchor was recovered in 1983. In 1987, NOAA completed baseline studies at the site that were essential for determining the rate of deterioration of the hull and changes in the Sanctuary environment.

In the 1990s NOAA began noticing an alarming pattern of accelerated deterioration in several areas of the wreck. In 1996, NOAA was given a mandate by Congress to come up with a plan to preserve the *Monitor.* In 1998, NOAA released a long range plan that outlined a six-step proposal for stabilizing portions of the *Monitor's* hull and recovering the vessel's steam engine and rotating gun turret.

The *Monitor's* nine-foot (three-meter) cast iron propeller and eleven feet (3.3 meters) of propeller shaft were recovered in 1998 with the help of the United States Navy. NOAA and the Navy began planning larger recovery expeditions in 1999, and implemented the stabilization portion of the plan in 2000 and 2001. In 2001 alone, more than 250 artifacts, including the vibrating lever steam engine, arrived at The Mariners' Museum in Newport News, Virginia to be conserved and prepared for exhibition at the USS *Monitor* Center.

The Monitor *propeller underwent six years of conservation. Today, the fully conserved* Monitor *propeller is on display at The Mariners' Museum in Newport News, Virginia. Photo credit: The Mariners' Museum.*

In 2002, a 41-day recovery effort culminated in the successful raising of the gun turret and two 11-inch (28-centimeter) Dahlgren smoothbore cannons from the ocean floor. The engine, cannons and gun turret are currently undergoing conservation at The Mariners' Museum.

In 2006, a team of researchers conducted a major mapping expedition to the *Monitor* to collect high-resolution digital still and video imagery which has been used to generate a high quality photomosaic of the site.

The turret breaks the surface for the first time in 140 years. Onlookers aboard the Emmanuel *cheer its arrival and marvel at a job well-done. Photo credit: Monitor Expedition 2002, NOAA/Ocean Exploration Program.*

Image compiled by Jeff Johnston of the Monitor *National Marine Sanctuary from a series of video stills. Although there is a distinct amount of distortion from the camera, this image shows some of the significant collapse that has occurred over the years. Photo credit:* Monitor *Collection, NOAA.*

Key species within the Sanctuary

Although the *Monitor* National Marine Sanctuary was primarily dedicated to the preservation of historical and cultural artifacts, a myriad of marine life also inhabits the areas surrounding the wreck. While some of these organisms are only passing through the Sanctuary, others live permanently within its boundaries, and some use the wreck of the *Monitor* itself as a habitat. As time passed after the sinking, encrusting organisms slowly started growing on the wreck which eventually attracted some larger animals and helped to develop a small ecosystem around the wreck site.

Because of the relatively small size of the *Monitor* National Marine Sanctuary, no marine mammals are permanent residents of the Sanctuary. However, a number of marine mammals do occasionally visit Sanctuary waters. These include bottlenose dolphins and fin, humpback and North Atlantic right whales.

Both bony fish and cartilaginous fish such as sharks, rays and skates live near or occasionally pass by the wreck of the *Monitor*. The fish found in the *Monitor* National Marine Sanctuary have diverse lifestyles and ecological roles: some live on encrusting organisms that cover the wreck or other fish, some live in nearby waters, and some only visit the wreck while passing through to other areas. Numerous fish species, including black seabass, oyster toadfish and great barracuda, call the *Monitor* home.

Abundant marine life and coral have made the Monitor *wreck home. Photo credit:* Monitor *Expedition 2002, NOAA/Ocean Exploration Program.*

Though not considered residents of the Sanctuary, loggerhead and leatherback turtles can sometimes be seen in the *Monitor* National Marine Sanctuary.

SAND TIGER SHARKS

Sand tiger sharks form large aggregations around shipwrecks and artificial reefs. These aggregations are unique along the east coast of the United States, and they, along with the shipwrecks around which they center, are the focus of an economically important recreational dive industry in North Carolina. Worldwide, populations of sand tiger sharks are considered "vulnerable" by the International Union for Conservation of Nature, and are listed as a "species of concern" by NOAA Fisheries Service. Sand tiger populations have been reduced by roughly 90% from the virgin condition by increased exploi-

A barracuda swims below while the Ocean Futures dive team completes their hour-and-a-half decompression after diving the Monitor. *Photo credit: Carrie Vonderhaar, Ocean Futures Society*

A sand tiger shark swims near the Monitor *wreck. Photo credit:* Monitor *Collection, NOAA.*

tation during the 1980s and 1990s. This species has been managed under the Highly Migratory Species Management Plan since 1997, however, the species continues to decline in abundance. Because individual sand tiger sharks possess unique spot patterns, scientists are able to conduct long-term monitoring studies of these animals using non-invasive photographic methods.

Emerging Environmental Issues

CONTINUING DETERIORATION

In 1998, NOAA submitted to Congress a Long-Range Preservation Plan for the wreck of the *Monitor*. In that plan, NOAA recommended that the *Monitor's* hull be stabilized and that significant hull components and artifacts be recovered before they completely disintegrated.

The hull has deteriorated to an alarming degree in recent years. Apparently, a major collapse of the aft lower hull occurred between 1987 and 1990, undoubtedly due to the weight of the boilers and machinery, which hung suspended from the inverted deck. The result was that the entire aft lower hull dropped several feet (a few meters) on the port side, bending or collapsing the remaining port deck support stanchions, until the weight of the machinery was taken up by the inverted deck and the underlying seabed. Also, probably during the same incident, the midships bulkhead partially collapsed, causing the turret support truss to separate from the bulkhead and cant to starboard.

The armor belt, constructed of wood covered by layers of iron armor, is also showing increasing signs of disintegration. A wood sample cored from the armor belt over the turret in 1998 was surprisingly sound and showed no evidence of shipworm damage. However, the stern end of the portside armor belt has deteriorated approximately six feet (two meters) since the wreck was discovered in 1974, and approximately 24 feet (seven meters) of the stern has disintegrated since the vessel sank in 1862. Hull plating can be seen lying in the sand at the stern of the wreck.

View across the forward area of the wreck looking aft. This image shows the significant collapse of the midships bulkhead. The structure to the right is the now displaced "turret support truss" and marks the original location of the Monitor's *turret. Photo credit:* Monitor *Collection, NOAA.*

USS *Monitor* Mosaic

Monitor Collection, NOAA

The Monitor's *armor belt is shown resting on its displaced turret, upside down. The armor belt is at the top of the photo. Photo credit:* Monitor *Collection, NOAA.*

The framing around the main engine. Photo credit: Monitor *Collection, NOAA.*

Deterioration of the USS *Monitor*

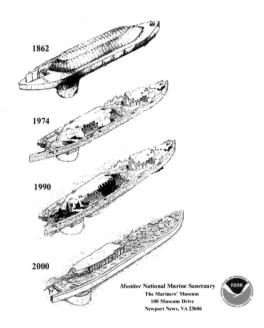

Illustrations showing the deterioration the Monitor *has undergone since the vessel sank in 1862. The rate of deterioration to the ship has increased markedly since 1991. Image credit: Islands in the Stream 2001,* Monitor *Collection, NOAA/Ocean Exploration Program.*

Permitted expeditions have noted even more significant changes at the site in recent years. The process of deterioration has begun to accelerate, with the *Monitor's* hull beginning to collapse like a house of cards. Most of these changes have occurred aft of the midships bulkhead. In 1990, an anchoring incident by a private fishing vessel damaged the wreck. The vessel's anchor snagged the skeg—the support for the rudder and propeller shaft—pulling it to starboard. This ripped open the hull plating at the stern, exposing the aft area of the engine room. It cannot be determined if this incident triggered the collapse of the lower hull.

The inverted deck is also beginning to show evidence of deterioration. Sunlight can be seen beneath the wreck where openings in the deck allow light to shine through onto the seabed. Most of the openings are believed to result from displaced hatch covers; however, others are the result of continuing deterioration. Iron armor plating has separated from the deck in several places, especially in the stern. At least one plate hangs from a few remaining iron spikes in the deck, with the other end resting on the sand beneath. Once the plating is gone, the underlying wood is quickly destroyed by shipworms.

Research within the Sanctuary

Since 1977, research at the *Monitor* site has been directed toward documenting the wreck in detail and understanding how it has been affected by natural deterioration and human activities. General research goals for the Sanctuary include the continued dissemination of historical and cultural information, the continued scientific study of the *Monitor* as an artificial reef, and the careful review and monitoring of privately-sponsored research activities in order to ensure that the site is protected and preserved.

- **Maritime archeology:** Archaeological research remains a major goal of the *Monitor* National Marine Sanctuary. With the majority of the *Monitor* wreck site unexcavated, the site remains a valuable repository of significant archeological information and historical material. Furthermore, the site is considered a gravesite and is listed as a National Historic Landmark. However, today the Sanctuary focuses on managing the site *in situ* to ensure the least impact on the site and surrounding environment Therefore, any future expeditions would document the wreck site for deterioration related to natural and human activities, conduct biological studies, and/or collect archaeological information through photos, videos and human observations.
- **Water quality monitoring:** The University of North Carolina at Chapel Hill (UNC) has been collecting data on water quality off Cape Hatteras for several years. Considering the proximity of the *Monitor* Sanctuary to the area of UNC research, the existing data may be applicable to the Sanctuary's waters. A partnership with UNC could be a starting point to establish the *Monitor* Sanctuary's own water quality monitoring plan in the near future. Parameters of particular interest include currents, temperature, salinity and pH, all of which affect deterioration rates of artifacts, as well as living resource conditions.

Two hard rubber US Navy buttons and a bone knife handle recovered from inside of the Monitor's *gun turret. Photo credit:* Monitor *Collection, NOAA.*

Visiting the Sanctuary

Note: In the last section of the book, "When You Visit the Sanctuaries," is detailed information about resources found within each sanctuary to help visitors have an enjoyable and productive visit.

The *Monitor* National Marine Sanctuary has always intrigued visitors because of its historic significance and remote location. The Sanctuary is important to researchers and archaeological investigation has been taking place ever since its discovery. There is much to be learned about the area. It is a difficult place to study on a regular basis in large part because of unpredictable and harsh offshore oceanic conditions.

View of the Monitor's *bow showing how the currents scour out around areas of the wreck.*
Photo credit: Monitor *Collection, NOAA.*

VISITOR'S CENTER

In 1987, The Mariners' Museum in Newport News, Virginia was designated the repository for USS *Monitor* artifacts and for their conservation and preservation. On March 9 2007, exactly 145 years after the historic clash between the *Monitor* and the *Virginia*, the USS *Monitor* Center opened at The Mariners' Museum. The $30 million, 63,500-square-foot facility serves as the primary visitor center for the *Monitor* National Marine Sanctuary.

Full-scale replica of the USS Monitor *outside the* Monitor *Center at The Mariners' Museum. Photo credit: The Mariners' Museum.*

The Monitor's *steam engine being restored at The Mariner's Museum. Photo credit:* Monitor *Collection, NOAA.*

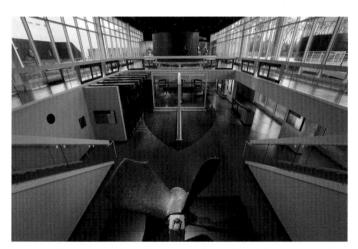

View of the Monitor *Center's large artifact gallery. Photo credit: The Mariners' Museum.*

Through an array of original artifacts, archival materials, immersive multimedia experiences and recreated ship interiors, visitors are transported back to 1862. The center is also home to the Batten Conservation Laboratory, a state-of-the-art facility where thousands of artifacts are being conserved and studied. Visitors to the museum can stand just feet from the *Monitor*'s two 11-inch Dahlgren guns and their carriages, the turret, and the steam engine. The conservation facility is open to the public during regular museum hours.

Highlights from the center include the *Monitor*'s iconic rotating gun turret and cannons, which were recovered in August 2002, and a full-size replica of the *Monitor* herself. The center's website[2] features several webcams, which allow people to view portions of the exhibit online.

2   http://www.marinersmuseum.org/uss-monitor-center/uss-monitor-center

In North Carolina, the North Carolina Aquarium on Roanoke Island, The North Carolina Maritime Museum in Beaufort and the Graveyard of the Atlantic Museum on Hatteras Island all have exhibits highlighting the *Monitor*'s history and her present status as an artificial reef.

The *Monitor* **National Marine Sanctuary office** is co-located with The Mariners' Museum at:
100 Museum Drive
Newport News, VA 23606

Telephone: 757-599-3122

BOATING

Monitor National Marine Sanctuary regulations prohibit anchoring, stopping, and drifting within the Sanctuary; conducting salvage or recovery operations; using diving, dredging, or wrecking devices; conducting underwater detonation; drilling in the seabed; laying cable; and trawling.

FISHING

Due to its location in the Gulf Stream, the *Monitor* Sanctuary is a popular destination for recreational fishing. Many charter boat captains take their clients to fish within Sanctuary borders. Live boat fishing is allowed within the Sanctuary, however, regulations restrict anchoring or drifting without the boat motor running. Recreational fishing is targeted at species such as black seabass, bank seabass, groupers, snappers, grunts and many others.

The USS Monitor *wreck, which sank on Dec. 31, 1862, now teams with marine life. Photo credit:* Monitor Collection, NOAA.

DIVING

Divers visiting sites may cause injury through poor diving techniques, inadvertently holding onto fragile artifacts or striking them with dive gear. To address this concern, the National Marine Sanctuary Program has developed a permitting system to allow divers access to the site while ensuring continued protection of the resource by placing a Sanctuary observer aboard. Permits can be obtained by applying through the *Monitor* Sanctuary office. [3]

---

3   http://monitor.noaa.gov/visit/permits.html

Research diver surveying the bow of the USS Monitor. *Photo credit:* Monitor *Collection, NOAA.*

Due to the great depth and unpredictable currents, the *Monitor* is inaccessible to most divers, although it remains popular with a small group of technical divers who use the necessary breathing gas mixes and procedures. Weather and sea surface conditions can be unpredictable at the *Monitor* so it is critical to have the most up to date weather information[4] before leaving shore. High seas and strong currents can make for very challenging dive conditions, not to mention queasy stomachs. For these reasons, the *Monitor* is not a good place for beginning divers.

---

4   http://monitor.noaa.gov/visit/weather.html

Rough weather and severe currents occur in the Monitor *National Marine Sanctuary difficult. Photo credit:* Monitor *Collection, NOAA.*

The USS Monitor *requires long decompression times. Ocean Futures Society's Blair Mott hangs on the deco-line before safely returning to the surface. Photo credit: Carrie Vonderhaar, Ocean Futures Society.*

When You Visit the Sanctuaries

Thunder Bay National Marine Sanctuary

Sanctuary Office

Thunder Bay National Marine Sanctuary
500 W. Fletcher
Alpena, Michigan 49707
Telephone: 989-356-8805
Fax: 989-354-0144
Email: thunderbay@noaa.gov
www.thunderbay.noaa.gov

Visitor Center

The visitor center for the Sanctuary is the Great Lakes Maritime Heritage Center, which is adjacent to the Sanctuary office. The Center consists of exhibits, theater, archaeological conservation lab, shipwreck artifact gallery, community boat-building center, scientific research facilities, and education space for special programs, meetings, and events.

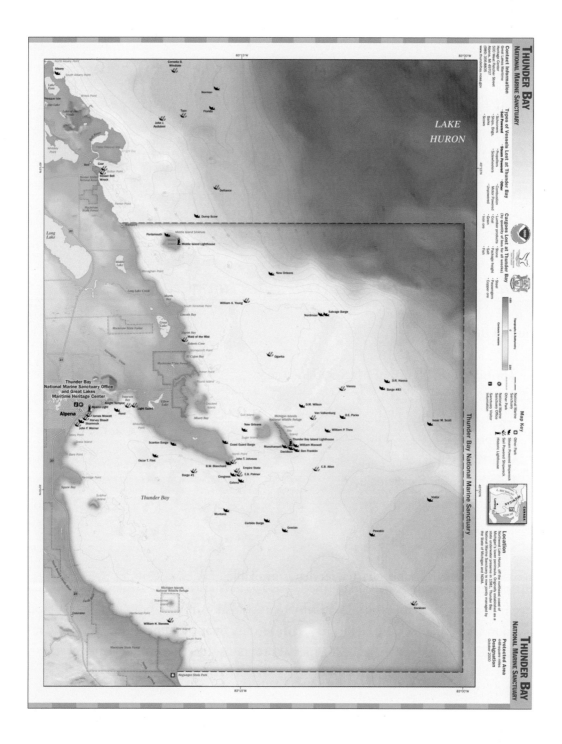

**Great Lakes Maritime
Heritage Center**
500 W. Fletcher Street
Alpena, MI 49707
Telephone: 989-356-8805
www.thunderbay.noaa.gov/maritime/glmhc.html

Chamber of Commerce

Alpena Area Chamber of Commerce
235 West Chisholm Street
Alpena, MI 49707
Telephone: 989-354-4181
www.alpenachamber.com

Air & Ground Transportation

Alpena is approximately 250 miles north of Detroit and 150 miles from Sault Sainte Marie, Saginaw and Traverse City, Michigan. The nearest airport is Alpena County Regional Airport (APN, www.alpenaairport.com), located six miles out of Alpena. Delta Connection provides daily scheduled airline service, including flights to Detroit Metropolitan Airport and Chippewa County International Airport, Sault St. Marie.

Aircraft Services

Full service FBO and charter service is available at Alpena County Regional Airport.

Aviation North
Toll Free: 800-572-3231

Rental Cars

Hertz	Telephone: 989-356-2414
Superior	Telephone: 989-354-0802
Enterprise	Telephone: 989-356-6960
Hudson	Telephone: 989-356-4641

Taxi/Shuttle

Alpena Cab	Telephone: 989-354-4601
Wheelz Cab	Telephone: 989-358-0245
Zimmers Shuttle	Telephone: 989-734-2255

Accommodations, Restaurants, Markets and Attractions

Because of the wide variety of commercial enterprises available to the public, we recommend that visitors check with area Chambers of Commerce for lists of local businesses in all categories, from where to stay to where to eat and what to do.

Diving/Snorkeling

Captain Mike's Dive Charters
7406 US-23 North, Suite B
Alpena, MI 49707
Telephone: 989-884-2722
Email: captmike@core.com
www.middleislandkeeperslodge.com

Great Lakes Dive Charters
146 Bear Point Road
Alpena, MI 49707
Telephone: 989-356-2908
Cell Phone: 614-581-9196
Email: fmrosinski@hotmail.com
www.greatlakesdivecharters.net

Great Lakes Divers
301 N. Third Street
Rogers City, MI 49779
Telephone: 989-734-7590
Email: steve@greatlakesdivers.com
www.greatlakesdivers.com

Great Turtle Diving & Sports, LLC
5316 W. Nicholson Hill Road
Hubbard Lake, MI 49747
Telephone: 989-324-7940
Email: gtds@provide.net
www.greatturtlediving.com

Thunder Bay Scuba
413 South Ripley Blvd
Alpena, MI 49707
Telephone: 989-356-6228
Email: Joe@TBScuba.com
www.tbscuba.com

UpNorth Charters
2961 Werth Road
Alpena, MI 49707
Telephone: 989-464-7241
www.upnorthcharters.com

Fishing

Bounty Hunter Fishing Charters
4029 El Cajon Beach Road
Alpena, MI 49707
Telephone: 989-354-3855
Cell Phone: 989-350-2168
Email: bountyhunterch@hotmail.com
www.bountyhunteralpena.com

Lake and Stream Fishing Charters
13395 Park Road
Lachine, MI 49753
Telephone: 989-379-2617
Cell Phone: 989-464-6436
www.fishalpena.com

Trout Scout Charters Licensed Fishing Charter & Guide Service
220 Richardson
Alpena, MI 49707
Telephone: 989-356-9361
Cell Phone: 989-657-2681
www.troutscoutcharters.com

Glass Bottom Boat/Shipwreck Tours

>Alpena Shipwreck Tours
>500 West Fletcher Street
>Alpena, MI 49707
>Toll Free: 888-469-4696
>info@alpenashipwrecktours.com
>www.alpenashipwrecktours.com

Kayak & Canoe Rental

>Green Planet Extreme Adventures Shipwreck Kayak
>400 E. Chisholm Street
>Alpena, MI 49707
>Telephone: 517-242-4752
>Email: greenplanetextreme@gmail.com
>www.greenplanetextreme.com

>Camper's Cove Campground & Canoe Livery
>5005 Long Rapids Road
>Alpena, MI 49707
>Toll Free (Reservations Only): 888-306-3708
>Telephone: 989-356-3708
>Email: info@camperscove.org
>www.camperscovecampground.com

Also, we recommend that you check the Internet or telephone directories for other possible listings.

Remember, if you can't find what you are looking for in these pages, contact the local area Chamber of Commerce for help. Even if they don't know the answer to your question, they will find it for you. Enjoy your Sanctuary visit.

Stellwagen Bank National Marine Sanctuary

Sanctuary Office

> **Stellwagen Bank National Marine Sanctuary**
> 175 Edward Foster Road
> Scituate, MA 02066
> Telephone: 781-545-8026
> Email: stellwagen@noaa.gov
> www.stellwagen.noaa.gov

Stellwagen Bank **does not** have a Visitor's Center.

A "virtual" visit to Stellwagen Bank, however, can be experienced at one of their exhibit partnerships. Each of these facilities in the Greater Boston and Cape Cod area hosts an exhibit about Stellwagen Bank, its environment, the marine life found there and its importance with the National Marine Sanctuary Program.

> Gloucester Heritage Maritime Center, Gloucester, MA
> www.gloucestermaritimecenter.org
>
> New England Aquarium, Boston, MA
> www.neaq.org
>
> Scituate Maritime & Irish Mossing Museum, Scituate, MA
> www.scituatehistoricalsociety.org/sites_maritime.html

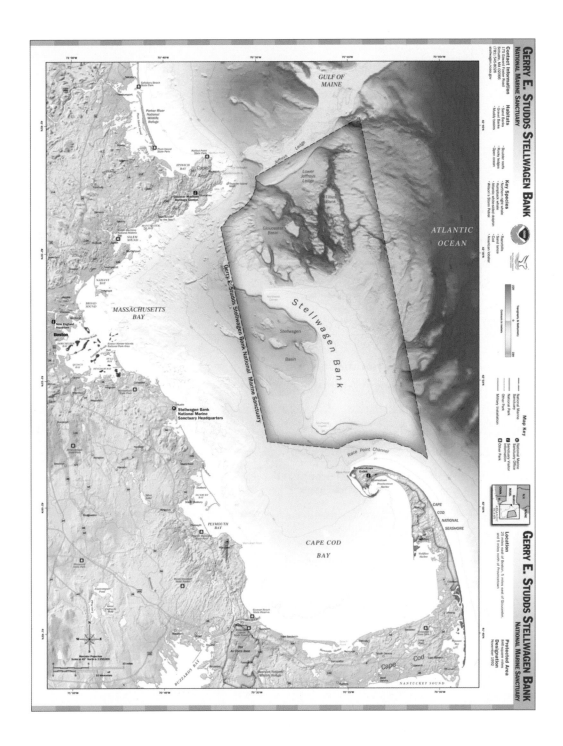

Cape Cod National Seashore Province Lands Visitor Center, Provincetown, MA
www.nps.gov/caco/planyourvisit/visitorcenters.htm

MacMillan Wharf Kiosk, Provincetown, MA
www.sanctuaries.noaa.gov/pgallery/pgstellwagen/human/human_19.html

Cape Cod Museum of Natural History, Brewster, MA
www.ccmnh.org

Woods Hole Aquarium, Woods Hole, MA
www.aquarium.nefsc.noaa.gov

Chambers of Commerce

Greater Boston Chamber of Commerce
265 Franklin Street, 12th Floor
Boston, MA 02110
Telephone: 617-227-4500
Email: info@bostonchamber.com
www.bostonchamber.com

Scituate Chamber of Commerce
P.O. Box 401
Scituate, Massachusetts 02066
Telephone: 781-545-4000
Email: info@scituatechamber.org
www.scituatechamber.org

Air and Ground Transportation

The major aviation gateway to the Stellwagen Bank National Marine Sanctuary area is Boston Logan International Airport (BOS, www.massport.com/logan-airport/Pages/Default. aspx).

> Logan International Airport
> 1 Harborside Drive
> Boston, MA 02128
> www.massport.com/logan-airport/about-logan/Pages/Default.aspx

Most major international airlines and many smaller regional carriers fly into Boston Logan International Airport. Visit the web site for full details of all available carriers and flights.

Rental Cars

Rental car agencies at the airport include Advantage, Alamo, Avis, Budget, Dollar, Enterprise, Hertz, National and Thrifty. Their contact information is available at www.visitingdc.com/car-rental/logan-airport-car-rental-companies.asp.

Taxi, Bus, Shuttle

Boston Logan International Airport has a handy Ground Transportation brochure which provides information about available services. Visit www.massport. com/logan-airport/Pages/Default.aspx and then the "To & From Logan" link for a detailed brochure.

Accommodations, Restaurants, Markets and Attractions

Because of the wide variety of commercial enterprises available to the public, we recommend that visitors check with area Chambers of Commerce for lists of local businesses in all categories, from where to stay to where to eat and what to do.

Diving

The following dive charters reported the availability of dive trips to the Stellwagen Bank National Marine Sanctuary and its surrounding waters:

Boston SCUBA, Inc
Boston Harbor Shipyard & Marina
256 Marginal Street
East Boston, MA 02128
Telephone: 617-418-5555
Email: js@bostondiving.com
www.bostondiving.com

Down Under Charters
4 Bonanza Road
Chelmsford, MA 01824
Telephone: 978-256-1208
Email: franlinnehan@gmail.com
www.downundercharters.com

Easy Diver
"J" Dock
Cape Ann Marina
75 Essex Avenue

Gloucester, MA 01930
Telephone: 978-525-3432
Email: info@easy-diver.com
www.easy-diver.com

Northern Atlantic Dive Expeditions, Inc.
Pickering Wharf Marina
23 Congress St.
Salem, MA 01970
Telephone: 617-480-5261
E-mail: info@northatlanticdive.com
www.northatlanticdive.com

Fishing

Because there is a very large number of charter fishing boats that service Stellwagen Bank, we chose to provide you access to the list maintained by the Massachusetts Division of Marine Fisheries. It is available online in the Massachusetts Saltwater Recreational Fishing Guide.   http://www.eregulations.com/massachusetts/fishing/saltwater/directory-charter-head-boats/.

Boating

The Sanctuary offers plenty of boating opportunity but boaters should avoid striking fishing gear, other boaters, and marine animals, such as whales, sea turtles, and basking sharks. There are numerous launching facilities for small boats nearby.

Whale Watching

Vessels from the whale watch operations below may travel into or near the Stellwagen Bank National Marine Sanctuary. For more information on whale watching trips, contact the companies directly. Many of these companies offer trained naturalists who provide commentary during the trips and collect data for on-going cetacean research programs.

Several of these companies participate in the Whale Sense program (www.whalesense.org), which is a voluntary education and recognition program offered to commercial whale watching companies (Maine through Virginia) by NOAA's Fisheries Service, NOAA's Stellwagen Bank National Marine Sanctuary and the Whale and Dolphin Conservation Society. The program was developed in collaboration with the Northeast whale watching community. Whale SENSE is a collaborative, voluntary program recognizing commercial whale watching companies committed to a responsible standard of whale watching.

Whale Sense participants are indicated by the logo after their name.

Cape Cod Departures:

Boston Harbor Cruises
MacMillan Wharf
Provincetown, MA 02657
Toll Free: 877-SEE-WHALE (877-733-9425)
Telephone: 617-227-4321
Email: contact@bostonharborcruises.com
www.bostonharborcruises.com

Dolphin Fleet Whalewatch
MacMillan Wharf
Provincetown, MA 02657
Toll Free: 800-826-9300
Telephone: 508-240-3636
www.whalewatch.com

Portuguese Princess Whale Watch
MacMillan Wharf
Provincetown, MA 02657
Toll Free: 800-442-3188
Telephone: 508-487-2651
www.princesswhalewatch.com

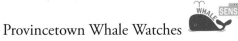

Provincetown Whale Watches
Fisherman's Pier
Provincetown, MA 02657
Toll Free: 800-225-4000
Telephone: 508-487-1102
Email: info@ptownwhalewatch.com
www.ptownwhalewatch.com

Hyannis Whale Watcher Cruises
Millway Marina
Barnstable, MA 02630
Toll Free: 888-942-5392
Telephone: 508-362-6088
www.whales.net

South Shore Departures

Andy Lynn Boats
Town Wharf
Plymouth, MA 02360
Telephone: 508-746-7776
www.andylynnboats.com

Captain John Boats
10 Town Wharf
Plymouth, MA 02360
Toll Free: 800-242-2469
Telephone: 508-746-2643
www.captjohn.com

Capt. Tim Brady & Sons
Town Wharf
Plymouth, MA 02360
Telephone: 508-746-4809
Email: tcbship874@comcast.net
www.fishchart.com

Boston Metropolitan-Area Departures

A.C. Cruise Line
290 Northern Avenue
Boston, MA 02110
Toll Free: 800-422-8419
Telephone: 617-261-6633
Email: bostonseaportboatcharters@gmail.com
www.accruiseline.com

Boston Harbor Cruises
Long Wharf
Boston, MA 02110
Toll Free: 877-SEE-WHALE (877-733-9425)
Telephone: 617-227-4321
Email: contact@bostonharborcruises.com
www.bostonharborcruises.com

Mass Bay Line Whale Watch
60 Rowes Wharf
Boston, MA 02110
Telephone: 617-542-8000
Email: info@massbaylines.com
www.massbaylines.com

New England Aquarium Whale Watch
Central Wharf
Boston, MA 02110
Telephone: 617-973-5206
www.neaq.org

North Shore Departures (including Cape Ann)

Cape Ann Whale Watch
Rose's Wharf, 415 Main Street
Gloucester, MA 01930
Toll Free: 800-877-5110
Telephone: 978-283-5110
Email: whale.watch@verizon.net
www.seethewhales.com

Captain Bill & Sons Whale Watch
33 Harbor Loop
Gloucester, MA 01930
Toll Free: 800-33-WHALE (800-339-4253)
Telephone: 978-283-6995
Email:info@captbillandsons.com
www.captbillandsons.com

Seven Seas Whale Watching
Seven Seas Wharf, 63 Rogers Street
Gloucester, MA 01930
Toll Free: 888-283-1776
Telephone: 978-283-1776
www.7seaswhalewatch.com

Yankee Fleet Whale Watch
Cape Ann Marina, Rt. 133
Gloucester, MA 01930
Toll Free: 800-WHALING (800-942-5464)
Telephone: 978-283-0313
www.yankeefleet.com

Newburyport Whalewatch
Hilton's Dock
54 Merrimack St.
Newburyport, MA 01950
Toll Free: 800-848-1111
Telephone: 978-499-0832
Email: info@newburyportwhalewatch.com
www.newburyportwhalewatch.com

Also, we recommend that you check the Internet or telephone directories for other possible
listings.

Remember, if you can't find what you are looking for in these pages, contact the local area Chambers of Commerce for help. Even if they don't know the answer to your question, they will find it for you. Enjoy your Sanctuary visit.

Monitor *National Marine Sanctuary*

Sanctuary Office

The Sanctuary office is co-located with The Mariners' Museum in Newport News, Virginia.

> *Monitor* **National Marine Sanctuary**
> 100 Museum Drive
> Newport News, VA 23606
> Telephone: 757-599-3122
> Fax: 757-591-7353
> www.monitor.noaa.gov/welcome.html

At The Mariners' Museum you can visit the USS *Monitor* Museum to learn all about the vessel, crew and military engagements. Extensive information is available at www.marinersmuseum.org/uss-monitor-center/uss-monitor-center.

Visitors to coastal North Carolina's Outer Banks have many opportunities to learn about the history of the USS *Monitor* and the National Marine Sanctuary System. The location of the shipwreck at 230 feet below the surface, however, does not allow for regular visitation, and **permits** are required to dive on the site, which is restricted to expert divers only.

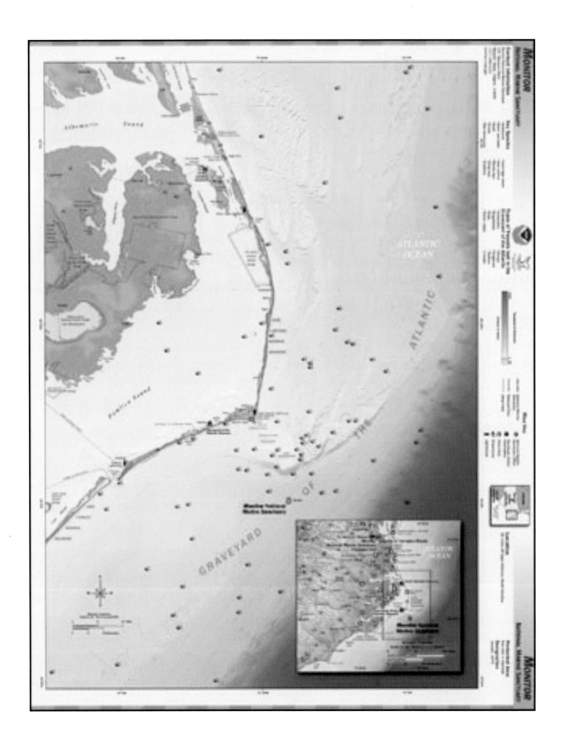

Chamber of Commerce

Hampton Roads Chamber of Commerce

500 East Main Street
Suite 700
Norfolk, VA 23510
Telephone: 757-622-2312
Fax: 757- 622-5563
www.hamptonroadschamber.com

Air and Ground Transportation

The **Norfolk International Airport** (ORF, www.norfolkairport.com) provides commercial and private aircraft access to the Hampton Roads area. It offers about 80 departures daily through American Airlines, Delta Air Lines, Southwest Airlines, United, and US Airways. The airport provides restaurants, shops and meeting space.

Aircraft Services
Full fixed base operator services are available:

Landmark Aviation
Toll Free Phone: 800-485-4041
Aircraft Charters: 800-548-1978

Rental Cars

Alamo	Toll Free: 800-462-5266
Avis	Toll Free: 800-831-2847
Budget	Toll Free: 800-527-0700
Dollar	Toll Free: 800-800-4000
Enterprise	Toll Free: 800-736-8222
Hertz	Toll Free: 800-654-3131
National	Toll Free: 800-227-7368
Thrifty	Toll Free: 800-367-2277

Bus/Shuttle

There is **no** bus service to and from Norfolk International Airport. Shuttle service is available between nearby cities and the airport.

> James River Transportation Airport Connection
> Toll Free: 866-823-4626
> Telephone: 757-963-0433

Taxi

Andy's Cab Co.	Toll Free: 866-840-6573
Black and White	Telephone: 757-855-4444
City Wide Cabs	Telephone: 757-857-5950
Duke Cab Co.	Telephone: 757-583-4079
East Side Cabs	Telephone: 757-718-0937
Eden Cab Co.	Telephone: 757-724-5555
Norfolk Checker	Telephone: 757-855-3333
Oceanside Executive	Telephone: 757-455-5996
Southside Cab Co.	Telephone: 757-423-0154
Waterside Taxi Co.	Telephone: 757-531-6430
Yellow Cab/Norfolk	Telephone: 757-857-8888

Newport News/Williamsburg International Airport (PHF, www.flyphf.com/content/)

Allegiant, Delta, Frontier, and US Airways have departures out of Newport News/Williamsburg Airport.

Aircraft Services

Corporate and general aviation aircraft at Newport News/Williamsburg International Airport are serviced by two full-service Fixed Base Operators.

Atlantic Aviation	Telephone: 757-886-5755
Rick Aviation	Telephone: 757-874-5727

Rental Cars

Avis	Toll Free: 800-331-1212
Budget	Telephone: 757-874-5794
Enterprise	Toll Free: 800-261-7331
Hertz	Toll Free: 800-654-3131
National	Toll Free: 800-227-7368

Bus

The airport is also served by the Hampton Roads Transit city bus system, which may be reached at 757- 222-6100.

Taxi

All City Taxi	Telephone: 757-380-8300
Associated Cabs	Telephone: 757-887-3412
Hops Cabs	Telephone: 757-245-3005
Independent Cab	Telephone: 757-245-8378
North End Cab	Telephone: 757-244-4000
Orange Cab Co.	Telephone: 757-369-8977
Yellow Cab	Telephone: 757-855-1111

Approved Private Cars (Limos)

Carey Transportation	Telephone: 757-853-5466

Chauffeured Sedan
Services, LLC   Telephone: 757-898-7172

Distinguished Executive
Transportation   Toll Free: 866-783-5192

Tidewater Coach/Williamsburg
Shuttle   Telephone: 757-218-9539

Williamsburg Chauffer
Service, LLC.   Telephone: 757-927-5049

Marrow Transit   Telephone: 757-564-5466

Chauffeured Transportation
Service   Telephone: 757-220-2257

Oleta Coach Lines   Telephone: 757-253-1008

Affinity Limousine   Telephone: 757-850-0089

Access Transportation
Corporation   Telephone: 757-723-5466

Cardinal Messenger   Telephone: 757-271-6208

Accommodations, Restaurants, Markets and Attractions

Because of the wide variety of commercial enterprises available to the public, we recommend that visitors check with area Chambers of Commerce for lists of local businesses in all categories, from where to stay to where to eat and what to do.

Diving, Fishing, Boating

Because of the unique nature and small size of this Sanctuary, diving, fishing, and boating are not activities allowed by the public. Sanctuary regulations prohibit anchoring, stopping, and drifting within the Sanctuary; conducting salvage or recovery operations; using diving, dredging, or wrecking devices; conducting underwater detonation; drilling in the seabed; laying cable; and trawling. Access is generally limited to scientific research conducted under a permit issued by NOAA; however, special-use permits are issued for non-research visits to this historic vessel. Contact the *Monitor* National Marine Sanctuary for more information.

Of course, the Outer Banks of North Carolina are renowned for a variety of diving, fishing and boating activities. Charter operators may be found through local Chambers of Commerce.

Also, we recommend that you check the Internet or telephone directories for other possible listings.

Remember, if you can't find what you are looking for in these pages, contact the local area Chamber of Commerce for help. Even if they don't know the answer to your question, they will find it for you. Enjoy your Sanctuary visit.

Acknowledgments

- The *Explore the National Marine Sanctuaries with Jean-Michel Cousteau* series would not be possible without the creation of the two-hour PBS television special, *America's Underwater Treasures,* co-produced with KQED Public Broadcasting in San Francisco, the companion limited edition book *America's Underwater Treasures*, and the talented people who contributed to those projects
- Julie Robinson, co-author *America's Underwater Treasures* Limited Edition Book
- The staff at Ocean Futures Society: Charles Vinick, Sandra Squires, Lida Pardisi, Laura Brands, Carey Batha, Jim Knowlton, Brian Hall, Nathan Dembeck, Matthew Ferraro, Carrie Vonderhaar, Nancy Marr, Marie-Claude Oren
- Ocean Futures Society's Dr. Richard Murphy, Director of Science and Education; Pam Stacey, Co-Producer and writer of the film *America's Underwater Treasures*; Don Santee, Chief of Expeditions, and Holly Lohuis, Expedition Biologist for reviewing and fact checking the manuscript
- All of the members of the *America's Underwater Treasures* expedition team for sharing their stories and allowing us to explore the sanctuaries through their eyes
- Dr. Sylvia Earle for her Foreword
- Fabien and Céline Cousteau
- Dr. Jane Lubchenco, Administrator, National Oceanic and Atmospheric Administration
- Daniel Basta, Director, National Marine Sanctuary System, NOAA

- Matt Stout, Communications Director, National Oceanic and Atmospheric Administration
- Sarah Marquis, West Coast/Pacific Media Coordinator, National Marine Sanctuary System, NOAA
- Reed Bohne, Regional Director, Northeast Region, National Marine Sanctuaries
- National Marine Sanctuary Superintendents, especially Jeff Gray (Thunder Bay), Craig MacDonald (Stellwagen Bank), and David Alberg (Monitor)
- National Marine Sanctuary Staff and Volunteers
- National Marine Sanctuary Foundation, Jason Patlis, President, and Lori Arguelles, Past-President
- Dr. Maia McGuire, Research Editor and Compiler
- Nate Myers, Cover Designs and Interior Layouts
- Sandra Sites, In-house Copyeditor

- And a special "Thank You" to Carrie Vonderhaar from the Ocean Publishing Team for her incredible assistance and coordination. She is absolutely terrific!

Glossary

Anemone, sea: a sea animal with a crown of tentacles at the top of a fleshy polyp or stalk; the tentacles contain stinging cells

Baleen: a tough, horny material growing in comblike fringes from the upper jaws of some species of whales; a horny keratinous substance found in two rows of transverse plates which hang down from the upper jaws of baleen whales

Ballast: a heavy substance placed in such a way as to improve stability and control (as of the draft of a ship or the buoyancy of a balloon or submarine)

Ballast tank: a tank in the hold of a ship that can be pumped full of or free from water ballast.

Bark: a sailing ship of three or more masts with the aftmost mast fore-and-aft rigged and the others square-rigged

Benthic: on or near the bottom of a lake, river or ocean

Breaching (whale): leaping out of the water

Brig: a 2-masted square-rigged ship

Cetacean: any of an order (Cetacea) of aquatic mostly marine mammals that includes the whales, dolphins, porpoises, and related forms

Demersal: living near, deposited on, or sinking to the bottom of the sea

Derelict (traps): abandoned by the owner. In the marine environment fishing gear is often moved or torn loose by storms, becoming derelict.

Dory trawling: a method of fishing from small boats using lines that had up to 1,600 baited hooks.

Extirpation: destroying completely

Fluke: one of the lobes of a whale's tail

Groundfish: a bottom fish; especially a marine fish (as a cod, haddock, pollack, or flounder) of commercial importance

Invasive species: aquatic and terrestrial organisms that have been introduced into new ecosystems throughout the United States and the world, both harming the natural resources in those ecosystems and threatening the human use of those resources

Keelson: a longitudinal structure running above and fastened to the keel of a ship in order to stiffen and strengthen its framework

Midden: a refuse heap

Pelagic: refers to animals that live in the open sea, away from the coast or seafloor

Port: the left side of a ship or aircraft looking forward

Portage: the carrying of boats or goods overland from one body of water to another or around an obstacle (as a rapids)

Remote sensing: the use of an instrument, such as a radar device or camera, to scan the earth or another planet from space in order to collect data about some aspect of it

Rig dragger: The eastern rig dragger is a wooden-hulled engine-powered fishing vessel that deployed, towed, and recovered its otter trawl net or dredge over the vessel's side as opposed to over the stern as done in modern stern trawlers

Schooner: a typically 2-masted fore-and-aft rigged vessel with a foremast and a mainmast stepped nearly amidships

Seine: a large net with sinkers on one edge and floats on the other that hangs vertically in the water and is used to enclose and catch fish when its ends are pulled together or are drawn ashore

Shipworm: any of various marine clams (especially family Teredinidae) that have a shell used for burrowing in submerged wood and a wormlike body and that cause damage to wharf piles and wooden ships

Sloop: a fore-and-aft rigged boat with one mast and a single jib

Stanchion: an upright bar, post, or support (as for a roof or a ship's deck)

Starboard: the right side of a ship or aircraft looking forward

Substrate: the base on which an organism lives

Trawl net: a large conical net dragged along the sea bottom in gathering fish or other marine life

Tunicate: any of a subphylum of marine chordate animals (also called ascidians) that are filter feeders having a thick secreted covering layer, a greatly reduced nervous system, and only in the larval stage a notochord

Windlass: any of various machines for hoisting or hauling

Zooplankton: planktonic organisms belonging to the animal kingdom, the majority of which are small crustaceans (copepods, krill), arrowworms, and gelatinous creatures that feed primarily on phytoplankton.

Index

Biographies

Jean-Michel Cousteau

Explorer. Environmentalist. Educator. Film Producer. For half a century, Jean-Michel Cousteau has dedicated himself and his vast experience to communicate to people of all nations and generations his love and concern for our water planet.

Since first being "thrown overboard" by his father at the age of seven with newly invented SCUBA gear on his back, Jean-Michel has been exploring the ocean realm. The son of ocean explorer Jacques Cousteau, Jean-Michel has investigated the world's oceans aboard *Calypso* and *Alcyone* for much of his life. Honoring his heritage, Jean-Michel founded Ocean Futures Society in 1999 to carry on this pioneering work.

Ocean Futures Society, a non-profit marine conservation and education organization, serves as a "Voice for the Ocean" by communicating in all

Photo Credit: Carrie Vonderhaar, Ocean Futures Society

media the critical bond between people and the sea and the importance of wise environmental policy. As Ocean Futures' spokesman, Jean-Michel serves as an impassioned diplomat for the environment, reaching out to the public through a variety of media.

Jean-Michel has received many awards, including the Emmy, the Peabody Award, the 7 d'Or, and the Cable Ace Award, and has produced over 80 films. Cousteau is the executive producer of the highly acclaimed PBS television series *Jean-Michel Cousteau: Ocean Adventures*. In 2006, more than three million Americans learned about the Sanctuaries for the first time from the award-winning film *America's Underwater Treasures*, part of the *Ocean Adventures* series. Also in 2006, Jean-Michel's initiative to protect the Northwest Hawaiian Islands took him to the White House where he screened, *Voyage to Kure*, for President George W. Bush. The President was inspired and in June 2006, he declared the 1,200-mile chain of islands a Marine National Monument—at the time; the largest marine protected area in the world.

Jean-Michel is also one of the founders of the National Marine Sanctuary Foundation and is currently a Trustee Emeritus.

Most recently, Jean-Michel and his Ocean Futures Society team were among the first to survey and film under water at the Gulf of Mexico Deep Horizon oil spill. Their footage was used as evidence that large masses of oil and dispersant were traveling under water.

The mission of Ocean Futures Society is to explore our global ocean, inspiring and educating people throughout the world to act responsibly for its protection, documenting the critical connection between humanity and nature, and celebrating the ocean's vital importance to the survival of all life on our planet.

JEAN-MICHEL COUSTEAU'S
OCEAN FUTURES SOCIETY

WWW.OCEANFUTURES.ORG

"Protect the ocean and you protect yourself"

Ocean Futures Society is a non-profit 501(c)(3) organization, U.S. tax ID #95-4455199

Dr. Sylvia A. Earle

Photo credit: Carrie Vonderhaar, Ocean Futures Society

Dr. Sylvia A. Earle is a longtime friend of Jean-Michel Cousteau and has been a member of the Ocean Futures Society Advisory Board since its beginning in 1999. She is a pioneer in ocean exploration and research and is currently an Explorer-in-Residence at the National Geographic Society, leader of the Sustainable Seas Expeditions, chair of the Advisory Councils for Harte Research Institute and for the Ocean in Google Earth. Dr. Earle also served as Chief Scientist of NOAA in the early 1990s and she is a 2009 recipient of the coveted TED Prize for her proposal to establish a global network of Marine Protected Areas. Dr. Earle is one of the founders of the National Marine Sanctuary Foundation and is currently a Trustee Emeritus.

Dr. Maia McGuire

Photo credit: Debbie Penrose, Florida School for the Deaf and Blind

Born and raised in Bermuda, Dr. Maia McGuire, Research Editor and Compiler for this book, has been the University of Florida Sea Grant Extension Agent for northeast Florida since 2001. She holds a BS in Marine Biology and a PhD in Marine Biology and Fisheries. Prior related experience was with Harbor Branch Oceanographic Institution. Dr. McGuire is an active member in several organizations, including the National Marine Educators Association, Florida Marine Science Education Association, and the Association of Natural Resource Education Professionals, among others. She has won several honors and frequently speaks at regional and national conferences.

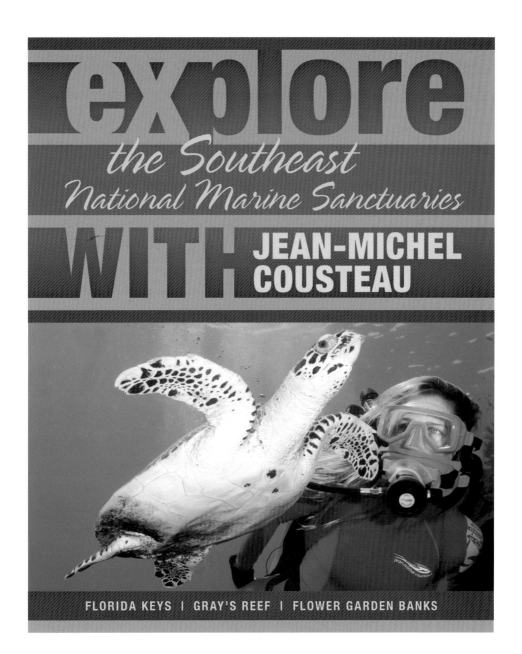

explore
the Southeast
National Marine Sanctuaries
WITH JEAN-MICHEL COUSTEAU

FLORIDA KEYS | GRAY'S REEF | FLOWER GARDEN BANKS

Available at all booksellers

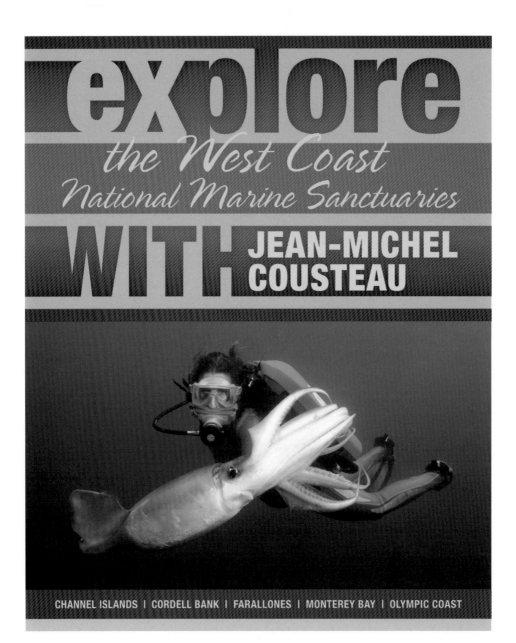

Available at all booksellers

explore
the Pacific Islands
National Marine Sanctuaries
WITH JEAN-MICHEL COUSTEAU

HAWAIIAN ISLANDS HUMPBACK WHALE / FAGATELE BAY / PAPAHĀNAUMOKUĀKEA MONUMENT

Available Fall 2013

Notes

Notes

Notes

Notes

Notes

Notes

Notes

Notes

Notes

Notes

Notes